HOW TO SURVIVE AUSTERITY

A Manager's Guide to
Doing More With Less and
Emerging as a Leader in
the New Public Sector

MIKE GILL

Praise

"Finally a book which not only provides practical and challenging new ways to face the ongoing and deepening pressures for public sector managers, but also reminds us that there is still much to cherish and preserve. A refreshing read which left an unfamiliar feeling of optimism."

Alice Benton, Lead Commissioner at NHS England and Cambridgeshire and Peterborough Clinical Commissioning Group (CCG)

"The policy of austerity, whether you consider it a necessary evil or a serious mistake, will be with us for some time. Mike Gill asks challenging questions about how to survive (even, he argues, thrive) if you're a manager in the public services."

Geoff Fimister, former Head of Newcastle City Council's Welfare Rights Service, writer and consultant with over 40 years' experience in the public, voluntary and private sectors

"All of us in the public sector will just have to get used to austerity. As Mike explains, we'll need to do things differently if we want to survive and thrive over these next five years. *How To Survive Austerity* offers valuable advice – best read it as soon as you can."

Mark Cockerton, Chief Executive of clinical out-of-hours providers across the UK and advisor to the Department of Health

"If you have ever been asked to deliver more for less, this book is your practical guide to help you do that in a thoughtful way that puts the impact of your services at the heart of your decision making."

Lucy Gower, Author of *The Innovation Workout*, innovation expert and Director at Lucidity

"Will I survive austerity? The simple answer is I am now better prepared, thanks to this publication."
Andy Vasey, HP Business Services Manager for Europe, Middle East and Africa

"Well structured and wonderfully readable – provides the tools and confidence that public sector managers need now more than ever."
Hilary Coyne, Major Projects and Change Manager at City of Edinburgh Council

"The book *How to Survive Austerity* provides not just clarity but solutions on how to deal with austerity – a word few understand the cause and effect of. If you are in the public sector or interested in how the economy works, this book is for you. It provides insights and a unique solution, to the reader's delight."
Darshana Ubl, entrepreneur, keynote speaker and SME advisor as seen on BBC News

"Austerity is a much used word these days, but in his book Mike Gill sets out the real impact of austerity on the public sector today. If you believe in public services, this is well worth a read."
Andrew Hartshorn, Managing Director at Methods Advisory Services

"As a public sector organisation, if you want the public to 'cherish' your service, you first have to CHERISH it and them. Use this rigorous, tested process to be the change you want to see and deliver remarkable results." 'Be the change you want to see in the world' (Ghandi)."
Ali Stewart, executive and leadership coach and author of the successful book, *Insights into Liberating Leadership*

RETHINK PRESS

First published in Great Britain 2016
by Rethink Press (www.rethinkpress.com)

© Copyright Mike Gill

Contents

Foreword

There is no magic secret to surviving austerity. However, this book offers a series of approaches to guide senior managers in the public sector through the greatest period of financial retrenchment since World War Two.

The public sector is shrinking by around 30% in a very short period of time. What took over 100 years to develop is being decimated on an annual basis in order to arrest the rate of increase in the national debt. But *all* of these efforts are undone by two things: the cost of servicing our £1.3 trillion debt and the increased cost of retirement pensions.

You have to be positive and realise the awesome consequences of *not* cutting public spending elsewhere.

Even the 'protected' Departments of Health, Defence and Education face severe financial restrictions. Gone are the days of squeezing the cuts target out of a large budget by spreading the jam more thinly. We are firmly in the territory of stopping doing things and drastically re-engineering those services we are lucky enough to retain.

This book is designed to help managers to respond to this challenge – but it will not be easy. The speed and scope of the retrenchment makes it difficult for any service to escape the closest scrutiny. It may be possible to argue that your services are more valuable or more essential than others, but the litany is of tough justice: equal misery for all. The scope for special pleading is very small.

As you work through the key defences suggested in this book, it may be tempting to think that the battle can be won or lost in one year – do not fall into that trap. Experience from those departments which have been seeking savings over the last parliament suggests that a ruthless approach works better than the traditional attempts to creep under the bar on a year by year basis. A more sustainable approach is to determine what the key 60 or 70% of the resource base you currently have will buy. Then try to make sure that the cuts are centred outside that irremediable core. But don't forget to scrutinise the core areas to within an inch of their lives. Nothing is sacrosanct. Otherwise you will end up in a place you don't want to be.

I wish you well on your journey.

Jim Brooks

Jim Brooks has over 30 years' experience in public sector management. He was City Treasurer of Manchester and Chief Executive at Borough of Poole and Kingston-upon-Hull City Council. He coaches and mentors chief executives and chief officers and is an Independent Board Member for the Department of Environment in Northern Ireland.

CHAPTER 1

Only Read This Chapter

What this chapter covers

- A brief summary of *How to Survive Austerity* and how it will help you survive the next five years.
- An overview of what the New Public Sector looks like and how you can emerge as one of its leaders.
- A summary of the seven essential steps of *How to Survive Austerity*: *a* practical method of preparing yourself and your service for the challenges ahead.
- Reasons (if you really need them) for *only* reading this chapter, but even better reasons for reading the rest of the book.

Why do I need *How to Survive Austerity?*

I wrote *How to Survive Austerity* for managers of public services across the UK with annual budget responsibility of between £5m and £20m. Do not worry if your responsibility falls outside this range. The techniques I provide in the book still apply to you.

You are the backbone of public service delivery. People up and down the country need your service. And now you face the greatest challenge you have ever faced in your career – because of this thing we call austerity. A New Public Sector will emerge from the significant changes being driven by austerity. And you need to be ahead of this 'opportunity curve'.

Austerity is everywhere, in this country, across Europe and beyond. Austerity trips off the tongues of newsreaders a hundred times a day. People have marched in the streets against austerity. But austerity takes different forms in different parts of the public sector and in different parts of the country. Whatever form it takes in your part of the public service, the key challenges you face are a drive to ensure vastly improved services, reduced – or even no – services, and inevitably, a lot less money.

As I was finishing writing *How to Survive Austerity*, the Chancellor of the Exchequer, George Osborne, had just finished delivering the conclusions of the 2015 Spending Review. Aside from unexpected changes to things like working tax credits, his speech on 25 November 2015 set out public sector budget cuts for some 'non-ring-fenced' departments of between 15% and 37%. Overall day-to-day departmental spending was cut by £20 billion – *equivalent to 0.8% of total expenditure each year by 2020.*

Those reductions were the culmination of many months of wrangling between the Treasury and spending departments. The ramifications for managers of services affected by those reductions will be severe and will be felt for years to come. Some of the key points of the 2015 Spending Review were that:

- State spending, as a share of total national output, will to fall to 36.5% in 2020, down from 45% in 2010.
- While the budgets of policing, health, education, international aid and defence remain protected, departments such as

transport, energy, business and the environment are among the biggest losers, with their respective resource budgets falling by 37%, 22%, 17% and 15%.

- Even within frozen budgets efficiency savings will be expected: police forces will be obliged to share resources, the NHS in England must find £22 billion in efficiency savings, and the Department of Health resource budget will fall by 25%.

- The 2015 Spending Review introduced a new social care 'precept' in council tax of up to 2% that will allow local councils to raise £2 billion for social care.

The term 'New Public Sector' is beginning to be used for the system and services that will remain post-austerity. That new term captures the nature and scale of the step changes that are occurring in the sector and describes the way things will be in the future. In *How to Survive Austerity*, I outline the leadership skills you will need to survive and thrive in that new environment.

Let us be clear. None of us actually asked for austerity in the first place. Of course, we know things went a bit wrong around 2008. And yes, it was not the public sector that needed all that bailout money. But that is in the past. Done. We all know balancing books is a good thing. And yes we all know the New Public Sector has to be efficient.

But as the announcement on the 2015 Spending Review demonstrates, the pressure on public service finances is severe, some would say un-precedented. Those pressures and the drive towards austerity challenge your claim to a future in public service. Austerity challenges the claims of your staff to a future in public service. And most impor-tantly, austerity challenges the very future of the service you hold dear and the delivery of services to people who really need them.

The Office for Budget Responsibility (www.budgetresponsibility.org.uk) – which I shorten to OBR throughout this book – is responsible for assessing how public finances are likely to evolve, based on existing government policies on tax and spending. Independent of government, the OBR estimates how much money the public sector will raise from taxes and other sources of revenue, and how much it will spend on things like public services, state pensions and debt interest.

In July 2015, following the Chancellor's budget, the OBR report *A Brief Guide to the UK Public Finances* said it expected UK PLC to raise £673 billion of income and spend £742 billion in 2015–16. That is a whopping deficit of almost £70 billion. And that is just an annual amount, in case you were wondering.

That is the deficit the Chancellor keeps talking about and the one he is keen to tackle. The key point for you is that closing that gap will affect the funding of most public services. Even services that are currently 'ring-fenced' and therefore, relatively insulated from the worst of the spending cuts, are not immune to efficiency plans. The impact on those services that are not ring-fenced will be severe, both for those receiving the services (the public) and for those who work in them (you and your staff).

It is certainly worth reading the OBR's independent report so you understand the implications of the 2015 Spending Review. It provides a no-nonsense update of the July 2015 report and leaves public sector managers in no doubt about the extent of the challenge ahead. You can find the report at:

www.budgetresponsibility.org.uk/efo/economic-fiscal-outlook-november-2015

How to Survive Austerity provides a means to prepare yourself and your staff through a practical, no-nonsense methodology you can start using today. A key aim is to help you present your service in the best way and emerge as a leader in the New Public Sector. *How to Survive Austerity* will make sure everyone understands what you do, how much it costs and why they should 'CHERISH' your service. CHERISH is a seven-step programme that can be rapidly applied to any service. It is particularly suited to the need to demonstrate improvement and public engagement.

But make no mistake: *How to Survive Austerity* is not a panacea. It will not magically save you from the ravages of austerity or from the drive to improve the outcomes of public services. What it will give you is the capacity you need to 'recognise your enemy', to understand why you need to make your service more visible and why you must make your service more relevant to the people you serve.

How to Survive Austerity provides you with the defensive tools you need to enable you to emerge as a leader in the New Public Sector. But the survival instinct is yours and yours alone. And it is your choice to apply what you learn from *How to Survive Austerity*. Or not.

What is the detail behind the methodology? Simply, the seven-step approach aims to make the public 'CHERISH' your service. I have used CHERISH deliberately to invoke the emotion and passion you should feel about your service. If you do not feel it, why should others care? The New Public Sector is typified by the public being more aware of what they are paying for and caring more about the services they truly value. The seven steps of *How to Survive Austerity* are shown in the following diagram:

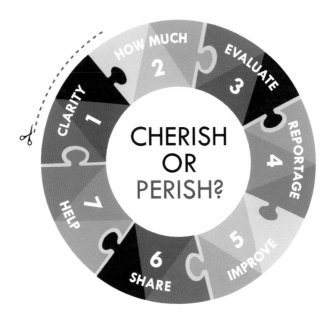

FIGURE 1: The seven stages of the CHERISH programme

Each of CHERISH's seven letters stands for a component part of a common sense technique for improving your service. The acronym serves as a simple way to remember what you are doing and to convey the message to others: 'I want you to CHERISH my service'.

By asking the public to CHERISH your service, you will go through steps leading to clarity, service improvement and cost reduction. All of those outcomes help you demonstrate to those looking for soft and easy targets that you have been brave. Not satisfied with the status quo, you have taken action. You have improved. And the outcomes of your actions are clear. You have embraced the future of the New Public Sector.

But remember that CHERISH rhymes with PERISH, neatly reminding us of what the likely consequence of inaction will be. CHERISH or PERISH.

When I was writing *How to Survive Austerity*, I imagined a 21st century Roman arena with an opportunity for a million or more 'thumbs ups' or a million or more 'thumbs downs'. The gladiators are you and the other public services, all fighting for survival. Those sitting in the 'Arena of Austerity' are the public. You will have to use all your skills and experience to be the last gladiator standing. And I will leave it to your own fertile imagination as to who is wearing the imperial purple toga and giving the final thumbs up or down of survival!

Keep the picture of an arena in your mind at all times and you will not go far wrong. To help you with that, I have made it even easier for you. Go to www.newpublicsector.com and you will find a ready-to-use virtual Arena of Austerity complete with people ready to CHERISH your services compared to other public services. Try it out and see what people think about your services.

What will *How to Survive Austerity* give me?

Like all good ideas, CHERISH is very simple. It is based on common sense. I do not deal in rocket science. It is jargon-free and does not need a management consultant to explain it and help you implement it. It is an approach you can deliver yourself.

The CHERISH methodology will help you to measure the value of your service against the best in the public and private sector, and to demonstrate that value. I provide some suggested tools in the book, and there are lots of free downloadable examples at www.newpublic-sector.com, along with handy links, articles and the latest news on austerity and public sector service improvement.

A brief description of each of the seven steps in *How to Survive Austerity* is shown below. Each step is explained in a separate section.

- **CLARITY** – Be clear about what your service delivers so the average person understands your message and cares about your service.
- **HOW MUCH?** – Identify the cost of your service and present it in a way the average person understands.
- **EVALUATE** – Develop a way for the average person to compare the cost of your service with others and judge whether you are offering great value.
- **REPORTAGE** – Devise ways to get your message out to the public and ask them the CHERISH or PERISH question.
- **IMPROVE** – Improve what you do based on the feedback from your Reportage stage and prepare an improvement plan that the average person would recognise as a promise to get better.
- **SHARE** – Connect your staff with the improvement plan so that each one of them becomes an ambassador for your service.
- **HELP** – Commit to supporting at least three other public sector services in the coming twelve months and help them deliver the same outcomes.

How much work will I need to put in?

For each of the seven steps, I provide examples and suggestions for:

- What you can do;
- How you can do it; and
- How you will know when you have done it right.

All the examples I provide are based on many years of working to improve the efficiency of public sector services and delivering transformation. And I have used that experience to project what the New Public Sector will need from its leaders. While the examples are practical, you need to apply them to your own service.

You must own your transformation process and you must hold a vision for making step changes to your services. Note that I did not say 'tinker with your services' or 'offer incremental improvements to keep the organisational efficiency plan at bay'. The New Public Sector demands you think about real transformation and improvement. *How to Survive Austerity* provides you with a clear framework, but you are responsible for making your service CHER-ISHed.

I will start our journey by exploring the scope of public services. What are they? How are they organised? Why are they under such attack? And I examine what people outside the public sector think about public services and those who work within them. That insight will enable you to understand the messages you need to develop to help you survive. I also provide an outline of what the New Public Sector will look like in five to ten years' time. At the time of writing this book, this can only be an outline based on what is likely to occur. It is certainly not a definition that will remain static, but it offers a

9

good starting point for any public sector manager tempted to view the current austerity drive as a temporary blip.

I am sure most managers of public services already know exactly what they deliver. And I am sure you already know how much your delivery costs. You have probably already benchmarked your service against others, using local, regional or national comparisons. I am certain you will also already have ideas for making your service better.

What you now need to learn is how to present that information in a way that the average person, unfamiliar with the language and systems of the public sector, can understand. The New Public Sector demands you find ways to engage with people, to excite, engage and capture the enthusiasm of the public. It is not an easy task, but it is something thousands and thousands of people in businesses big and small do every single day. You need to become one of those people.

You need to make sure your message gets out to government too. In this book I will often refer to 'government'. I use that term to encompass all the different arrangements we now have in different parts of the country, since Scotland, Northern Ireland and Wales already have different arrangements from England. Recent developments in the North of England are beginning to introduce greater devolution as part of the 'Northern Powerhouse' agenda; and different parts of the public sector report to government in different ways.

All those arrangements mean that the impact arising from the 'austerity agenda' will vary depending on where you are and what kind of service you are. But the core message is the same. Wherever your 'government' is, you must impress them as much as you have sought to impress the public. Make sure they understand what you do, how much you cost and how you will deliver improvements.

You can compare the government's role to that of the shareholders of a business. Those ultimate 'owners' of the business can, mostly, make decisions without recourse to, or consultation with, that business. Every business has customers who may like or dislike decisions made by a company and who make choices following a company decision. In the same way, government takes into account public reaction to decisions it takes.

Shareholders enjoy being informed about how their business is being run; it helps them make informed decisions. But shareholders can make illogical decisions if they are poorly informed. History is littered with some great examples: these may be decisions that the business may not like, or did not expect, and that their customers do not support. Government is not so different in its decision-making, so you will need to make sure all decision-makers receive good information about your service. The New Public Sector will mean the system is significantly leaner than the sector in the past. It will involve increased emphasis on real improvement as well as real public engagement.

So *How to Survive Austerity* will ask you to be brave. It will challenge your traditional thinking and ask you to apply what you already know in a different way. It will encourage you to view your service through the eyes of others. *How to Survive Austerity* will ask you to pitch your service in a way you probably have not done before, through clear and succinct messages. It will ask you to consider how you can best position yourself as one of the leaders in the New Public Sector.

11

So how much effort will you need to put in? Well, the good news is that you should already have most of what you need at your finger-tips. You should already have an idea of how to improve what you deliver and how you deliver it. That will make the rest easier. If you have not got those things – well, you are going to have to work a bit harder. But do not worry: *How to Survive Austerity* will help you through that learning too.

What will you get out of it? Well, you are likely to learn new tech-niques and new approaches. You will become acutely aware of what other people, outside the public sector bubble, think about you and your service. It may not sound comfortable, but it is better than the alternative.

What happens if you do not want to bother with all that effort? 'Let the future come to me.' 'There is nothing I can do.' 'What difference will it make?' Well, that is a choice you have to make for yourself. You can either roll over and let the future happen to you, or try to influence it.

One final point you might want to think about. Other public service managers like you will be reading *How to Survive Austerity*. They will be applying the same approach I am giving you. In the 'dog-eat-dog' environment that austerity generates, and that will typify the New Public Sector, can you afford not to be doing what they are doing?

I am pretty sure you will decide you cannot afford not to read *How to Survive Austerity*. I hope I have made a good case for not only reading this chapter. If you want a simple technique to maximise your chances of having a career in public services in five years' time, read on.

CHAPTER 2

Public Services – Setting the Scene

What this chapter covers

- The context of public services and why they are needed.
- People's opinions of the services they receive and their views on the people who provide them.
- A view of the future and of the risks posed to public services by the austerity agenda.
- The development of the New Public Sector and what it will take to emerge as a leader in it.

What are public services?

Wikipedia defines a public service as 'a service which is provided by government to people living within its jurisdiction, either directly (through the public sector) or by financing provision of services'. Those of us working in the public sector often do not stop to think about that description. We spend even less time trying to figure out what people outside the sector think about us, how they perceive our actions and what conclusions they reach about 'public servants'.

The public service part of our economy touches every part of our lives, from the emptying of our bins at a local level, the defence of our realm on a global stage, the social services provided to the most vulnerable, through to open heart surgery and assurance of the cleanliness of the restaurants we eat in. Some services, such as the police and the education system, are very visible. Others, such as safeguarding children at risk, preventing neighbours from building monstrosities and ensuring financial probity, are invisible apart from when they go catastrophically wrong.

If we think about the public sector in the same way we think about the financial sector or the industrial sector, we start to recognise that a single system or definition cannot be easily applied.

So when I talk about the 'public sector' in *How to Survive Austerity*, I am not only referring to the aggregate of services provided and funded by UK PLC but also, and more importantly, to the thousands of individual delivery units that make up the public sector. I think it is much easier to think about individual services and their respective costs and outcomes rather than just 'the sector' as a whole. We will return to the difficult 'middle bit' of the organisations that comprise the public sector a little later.

But let us start with a history lesson. Public services have been around in the UK a lot longer than people probably think – since as long ago as 1597, in fact. In that year, the Act for the Relief of the Poor established a system for collecting contributions and distributing clothes and food to the poor. Some would say little has changed in our society since then.

State education and old age pensions both came into being before the First World War, and most municipalities also provided varying degrees of public services well before universal access to a national welfare scheme. You have only to look at the many great examples of town halls up and down the land built during Victorian times – of which many are still in use.

What most people have in mind when they think about the start of public services is the rapid expansion in welfare services that came into being after the Second World War. The launch of the National Health Service and the National Assistance schemes in 1948 were aimed explicitly at tackling the five giants of 'want, disease, idleness, squalor and ignorance'.

While the focus of the public sector has changed somewhat since then, those core giants remain to some degree today. And the scope, scale and financing have increased too. The OBR website (www.budgetresponsibility.org.uk) will provide you with lots of links to a more detailed history of the rise of public sector since 1947 if you want it, but the brief version is:

- The public sector has got much bigger.
- The public sector has got much more complex.
- Public sector productivity has not kept pace with increases in the rest of the economy.

This latter point is important. It is one of the most frequent criticisms of the public sector by those outside it as well as by a great many within it. The perceived poor performance of the public sector makes it an easy target for detractors, and an easy target for politicians too. The New Public Sector will seek to alter that perception, although it is clear the journey will be difficult for the public sector and the public alike.

So what are the basic facts and how much has public sector spending increased? The following graph shows the annual proportion of

Gross Domestic Product (GDP) that has gone to public sector spending, using figures provided by the Office for National Statistics.

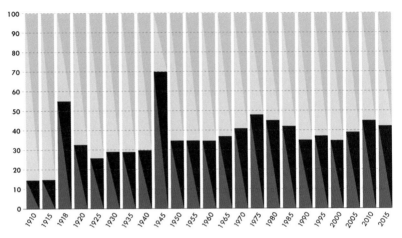

FIGURE 2: Public sector spending as a % of GDP
(Source www.ons.gov.uk)

That growth has established people's relationship with, and expectations of, what the state provides. But the current focus on austerity is changing all that. The OBR website, among others, provides the most up to date reports on the actual position and projections. It sets out what the New Public Sector will have to deliver and the significant structural and systemic shifts that will have to occur in order to support future service needs.

The £20 billion reduction in spending arising from the 2015 Spending Review attests to the extent of those shifts.

What public services do we need?

Many would argue that the scope of public services has altered radically from the vision shared by the architects of the welfare state in Britain. The benefits provided by the National Assistance Scheme were envisaged as a support to be called on in extremis, not as an entitlement that absolves the individual of any personal responsibility for their own maintenance. Proponents of a smaller state sector emphasise this.

An obvious difference between the public sector of the 50s and 60s and the public sector now lies in who is actually delivering these services. Most big nationalised industries, publicly owned for decades, have returned to the private sector. A host of other services that we once took for granted would be delivered by the public sector, such as street cleansing, refuse collection, drug rehabilitation and forensic services, are now provided by private or voluntary sector organisations. Many functions of government are now delivered under contract with private sector organisations. But all are still described as being public sector services. And each part of Britain provides a different picture. Contrast the local authority landscapes of, for example, London and Scotland and you start to understand key differences in the way services are organised in different parts of the country.

People often decry the state of our roads or rubbish collections and invoke 'third-world countries' as a benchmark for unsatisfactory services. In fact, conditions in these countries make it very clear to us why we need public services. On balance, most of us would probably not swap abolition of income tax for unmade-up roads and no ambulance service.

But when it comes to comparisons, we should at least make them with countries that purport to offer some level of public service rather than countries that are not in a position to offer any. The Institute of International and European Affairs (www.iiea.com) and the Organisation for Economic Co-Operation and Development (www.oecd.org) are great sources of data on different employment patterns in different parts of Europe and beyond.

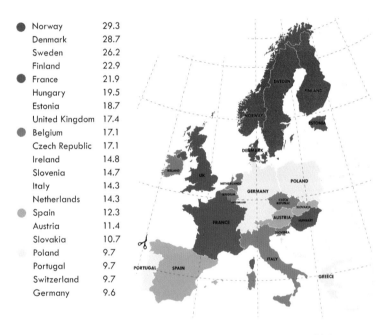

Norway	29.3
Denmark	28.7
Sweden	26.2
Finland	22.9
France	21.9
Hungary	19.5
Estonia	18.7
United Kingdom	17.4
Belgium	17.1
Czech Republic	17.1
Ireland	14.8
Slovenia	14.7
Italy	14.3
Netherlands	14.3
Spain	12.3
Austria	11.4
Slovakia	10.7
Poland	9.7
Portugal	9.7
Switzerland	9.7
Germany	9.6

FIGURE 3: European public sector employment %, 2011
(Source www.iiea.com)

So where does the UK sit? The diagram above uses data from the Institute of International and European Affairs and shows the UK sitting somewhere towards the middle of a spectrum that has the Scandinavian countries at the top, with their renowned enthusiasm for paying taxes that allow for high levels of public spending, and Greece at the bottom, despite the commonly held view that almost everyone in Greece works for the government. In Scandinavian countries almost a third of employees work for the government, compared with 17% in the UK. (Note, though, that these figures are for 2011, the latest available. A lot of change will already be in the system so it is well worth watching www.iiea.com and www.oecd.org for updates.)

What would happen if we did not have public services? Well much depends on the national consensus around a minimum standard of living, and on government fears of the UK replicating the civil unrest seen in countries where this consensus has been breached. Horror stories from the Greek financial crisis convey all too vividly the trauma of citizens in advanced economies who find their services and safety nets whipped away from under them.

What we think about our public services

To help me write this book, I undertook a simple survey to gauge the views of a range of people on how they perceived the public sector. I asked people outside the public sector and those who had never worked in it what they thought. I asked people working in the public sector who had not worked outside it what they thought. And I asked people working in the public sector who had previous outside experience what they thought. You get the idea.

I then undertook a number of more detailed discussions with some of those people to explore their views, all of which was designed to help me develop a model and benchmark that we can use during the CHERISH journey.

My survey and the benchmarks do not claim to represent a definitive nor scientifically derived conclusion. This was a survey designed to give an idea of what people think about the public sector. The outcomes are yardsticks you can think about when you are making improvements, and you will no doubt have views of your own you can add.

The model has been informed by the views of many kind people who took the time to complete my survey and talk to me. I have made sure the people and the comments they provided are not directly attributable, but here is a representative sample of who those people were:

PUBLIC SECTOR

Fraser	Involved in the audit of public services in Scotland
Alice	Responsible for an annual NHS commissioning budget of nearly £1 billion
James	Involved in the transformation of local government services in London
Jan	Involved in delivering support to the public in a large central government department

PRIVATE SECTOR

John	Involved in managing one of the UK's largest car manufacturing businesses
Andy	Responsible for the delivery of IT services across Europe, the Middle East and Africa
Martin	Involved in UK-wide investment and the development of technology ventures
David	Involved in the operational research in one of the UK's biggest leisure and insurance companies

FIGURE 4: Sample surveyed about the current public sector

So here we have a reasonable cross-section of roles and of industry sectors that will suffice for the purposes of developing a comparison model. All have more than ten years' experience in their sector. Some of those in the public sector also had private sector experience before they joined the public sector.

I have taken the conclusions of my survey and combined them with responses received during more in-depth conversations. While the main outcomes are discussed below, I will return to the comments they made throughout the book.

Topic 1 – Quality of public sector services

First, I asked about the perceived quality of public sector services and if it was getting better or worse. As you could perhaps anticipate, private sector respondents thought the quality was poor and getting worse while public sector respondents thought it was pretty good, if static. Interestingly, public sector respondents thought that austerity was being used as a tool to drive through difficult changes. They also thought those changes were more likely to happen than without austerity.

Opinion about what should be done about improving quality drew an interesting split between those in the public sector and those in the private sector. Private sector respondents universally mentioned generic issues such as reducing bureaucracy and red tape. However, public sector respondents were much more specific and mentioned better application of community involvement, better understanding of what the public really wanted and greater user participation in service design and decision making. Other key issues mentioned by all respondents included simplifying and systemising complex processes as well as better sharing of public assets and resources.

So more realistic solutions, or at least some of them, seem to lie within the public sector. Deeper exploration of the qualitative issues reveals deep-rooted systemic complexity and organisational protectionism rather than lack of ability as the real barriers to improving public sector quality. Put simply, the public sector must become better at developing more streamlined ways of doing things that place the public at the forefront of designing services. Those not involved in the sector tend to abbreviate that to 'cut bureaucracy'.

This will be hardly rocket science to most of those working in public services. But your ability to deliver this in the face of organisational complexity is likely to be what blocks your progress. The New Public Sector and the conclusions of the 2015 Spending Review will mean an even greater need to deliver change more quickly with less. Leaders will therefore need to become even better at managing their own organisational expectations and demands as well as those of the public.

Topic 2 – Cost of public sector services

Next, I asked for views on costs. All the private sector respondents thought public sector costs were too high, while all those in the public sector thought costs were about right or cheap for what they delivered. All respondents agreed there was a much greater need for the public sector to understand its costs better and to be able to explain them more clearly to the public.

All respondents commented on the need for investment in greater simplification and in better systems (both IT and non-IT) in order to drive down costs. But only those working in the public sector highlighted the systemic changes that have resulted in poorer information being available to public sector managers. The examples of changes to the NHS in particular were cited as delivering less clarity to managers on their budgets and costs. While the drive to reduce overall costs may have been successful, managers within the NHS have much less certainty than they once did about budgets and costs – not what the changes were designed to deliver, I am sure.

My respondents highlighted the need for all organisations to be clear about indirect costs, overheads and corporate costs. But the public sector managers were much more specific. They highlighted a significant lack of clarity in the provision of true service costs, meaning that managers are not only unclear themselves about real costs, but they are unable to provide a true picture to the public. Neither of those issues is likely to go down well in a period of austerity, when all costs are under scrutiny.

Topic 3 – Reporting on the performance of public sector services

The final area I probed related to performance reporting and informing the public about how well its public services were doing. Unsurprisingly, I had a real mix of responses on that topic, ranging from a 'total lack of useful information' to 'good quality reporting in some circumstances'. Even the latter comment, representing the more positive end of the spectrum of responses, was not exactly glowing – and not likely to find much favour with the public in the New Public Sector.

Our earlier exploration of what makes up the 'public sector' goes a long way to explaining the range of responses. By way of example, local authorities have a number of areas they are required to report on (which vary considerably in their nature and scope depending on where the authorities are). However, some respondents felt that while some aspects of local authority reporting were good, not all services were clearly explained and the value of the authority as a whole was not clear. At the other extreme, respondents had no clear idea about how some services were performing, with NHS services and central government services being mentioned most.

UK PLC does a good job (via the OBR) of explaining where the very large chunks of money go, but less so when explaining what value we get out of them. The nature of public services makes this meaningless as well as near impossible. But respondents were clear that the lower down the spending tree you go, the more information should be available. And not everyone has the time or inclination to delve into the OBR website or the annual reports of their local authority or acute hospital.

The message from the survey

So the message was that the public sector must become much better at presenting performance information in a more accessible way and in a way that is truly meaningful to the public, allowing the public to decide if services are offering good value for money.

Respondents gave examples of where the public sector is good at presenting information, generally when it is compelled to do so by competition. Some sections of the education market in some parts of the country were cited as examples of publicly funded bodies offering similar services competing with each other for clientele. So it can be done!

Respondents stressed that the public sector is very poor at making cost comparisons between its own services and those offered by the private sector. Acknowledging that the public sector has probity and procurement obligations, public bodies should not shrink from making comparisons, or from making those comparisons public, according to respondents. So the key issues I derived from this small survey to develop a model for the New Public Sector are:

- Those within the public sector tend to be more critical and more specific than those in the private sector about the key issues and challenges that need to be addressed to improve quality, costs and performance.
- The private sector is clear that the public sector must reduce its bureaucracy and must be much more accountable for the services it delivers, adopting private sector norms of informing and engaging with its customers.
- There is a clear need to involve the public more in the design, development and operation of public services, so that they feel they have greater control over the services they pay for.

These three key issues should not come as a great surprise to most public sector managers. But throughout the CHERISH journey, we will come back to those key issues and use them as a benchmark for our planned improvement actions. Although each service will vary, often dramatically, there can be little argument that all public sector managers will aspire to be efficient, relevant and wanted, even if the services they provide are stipulated by law, regulation or by civil need.

How great is the threat we face?

The recent rapid growth of the public sector is only one of the factors driving austerity; it is not the only reason. In order for the Government elected in May 2015 to meet its manifesto commitment to balance the country's 'books' over the lifetime of the Parliament, we needed something in the order of £42 billion to come out of public spending. A budget in July 2015 made changes to taxation meaning that that figure went down to something like £18 billion of reductions – still a massive amount, but the reduction from the original figure is at least recognition that public services still play an important role. And of course, that was followed by the Chancellor's statement on 25 November 2015 on the conclusion of the 2015 Spending Review. As I mentioned in the opening chapter, the Chancellor's speech on 25 November 2015 set out a reduction in overall day-to-day departmental spending of some *£20bn each year by 2020*, reducing state spending, as a share of total national output, to 36.5% in 2020, down from 45% in 2010.

While budgets in policing, health, education, international aid and defence remained protected, Whitehall departments such as transport, energy, business and the environment were the big losers, with their respective resource budgets falling by 37%, 22%, 17% and 15%. Scottish day-to-day revenue spending was reported to be down by nearly 6%.

So not a great picture across most of the public sector, and many commentators claim that changes to global circumstances render some of the Chancellor's assumptions about tax receipts and the recovery of the UK economy over-optimistic. While there is a clear plan, the reality and outturn are still a little difficult to predict.

Though issues associated with welfare payments, tax credits and the introduction of the living wage tend to grab the headlines, the reductions cited in the 2015 Spending Review in direct spending in departmental budgets for public services are likely to mean huge cuts in the staffing and operations of government departments, town halls, police and health services across the country.

Those headline-grabbing decisions relating to welfare payments, tax credits etc. have also been counterbalanced by the introduction of a 'productivity agenda', an old term which we will revisit in later chapters of the book. Productivity aims to make better use of what resources we have at the most basic level. And productivity is a word much used in other sectors of the economy, including the industrial and financial sectors.

In those sectors, large-scale investment in technology, equipment and process engineering has led to significant increases in levels of per-employee productivity. That increase in productivity often results in fewer employees working directly on individual processes, products or services. But in the private sector, such improved productivity and efficiency often leads to innovation and price reductions that, in turn, lead to increased demand for goods and services. So productivity often leads to greater employment and employers often shift resources to target new sectors or products, and the whole cycle starts again.

Public services tend not to follow that economic model, so 'productivity' in our context has a different meaning and different implications. There are many excellent books on economics – this is not one of them. If you are keen to learn more about the difference between public sector and private sector economics, drop me an email and I can try to point you in the right direction.

So we have ahead of us at least five years of restricted spending on public services, coupled with a 'carrot' of improving productivity in the wider economy. But the prospect of the public sector growing once things get brighter in the wider economy is wishful thinking. Those involved in delivering public services are best advised to get used to an increasingly challenging environment.

The New Public Sector will need to take that environment into account. The austerity programme is radically different from some of the efficiency programmes we have seen in the past. Market testing, outsourcing, the creation of executive agencies and auctioning national assets may have seemed a bit harsh, particularly if you happened to be working in the public sector. But such programmes were generally consensual, although competitive tendering for local government services in the 1980s and 1990s did not appear too consensual at the time. Today's message, and one likely to be with us for the foreseeable future, contains an underlying message of 'just because you are delivering a good service does not mean you will not suffer cuts'.

So the model for the New Public Sector will be different for a number of reasons:

- First, there is unlikely to be a rapid (if ever) return to 'business as usual' when the wider economy bounces back. Current government thinking appears to focus on 'reduce and eliminate' to a point that could permanently change the nature of public service.

- Second, those services that do remain will need to demonstrate a much greater connection with the public to survive. Note the use of the term 'connection' rather than the rather wider term 'engagement'. Service managers will need to develop better and more rapid ways of directly connecting with service users from within their organisational communications frameworks, so there will be a need for much better thinking and execution at both the strategic level and at the operational/service level. And that twin focus means less need for anything in the middle, as that level often delivers little, costs a lot and impedes progress.

- Finally, the drive to reduce costs means each service manager will need to be able to acquire effective services to deliver their outcomes within the deadlines and to budget. Those services may no longer be provided from within the organisation but, as always, they will need to comply with strategic, corporate and governance requirements. What this entails is empowering managers appropriately, so that they can make purchasing decisions that will see their desired outcomes being delivered.

FIGURE 5: Emerging model of the New Public Sector

What these issues mean in reality is expressed in the simplified diagram on the previous page. This represents what the New Public Sector is likely to mean for many public sector managers. A more detailed description of the New Public Sector can be found at www.newpublicsector.com.

As the diagram on the previous page demonstrates, as a public sector manager, you are subject to a government with an electoral mandate to make draconian cuts to address austerity, no matter what part of the country you are in and whether you are part of a service funded by a devolved or centralised budget. The extent to which the New Public Sector will affect different services in different parts of the country is difficult to predict right now.

I have mentioned the conclusion of the 2015 Spending Review, which has resulted in greater pressure on non-'ring-fenced' services but did not leave 'ring-fenced' services such as education, health and international development immune to cuts and their own future efficiency plans. For example, the Five Year Plan for the NHS in England has fairly draconian spending reductions factored into it.

We know this is the programme for the term of this Parliament. But what happens afterwards? As the New Public Sector diagram on the previous page outlines, there is unlikely to be a return to normality any time soon, if at all. The OBR's half-yearly *Fiscal Sustainability Report* (June 2015) highlighted the ageing population as the key challenge for the country in the years ahead. The report highlighted the economic impact of having more older people living for longer, with rising health and social care costs. It sets out the need for a redistribution of public spending, away from direct services into supporting people in the community. At this stage it is hard to imagine how the future norms of the New Public Sector will compare with today's provision of public services.

Read the OBR's report of November 2015 and see what impact it thinks restricting spending will have on its original assessment.

The headlines regularly talk about the gap between health and social care when older people leave hospital. When people no longer need clinical care hospitals, under pressure from a shortage of beds seek to move them off their premises to accommodation where they can receive more appropriate care. Except that 'more appropriate care' is now increasingly difficult to find. Older people often need more support but mostly do not need to be in hospital. And if you think the need for care and funding to pay for it is massive now, read the OBR's June 2015 report. This provides some frankly eye-watering estimates of what the economy needs to generate over the next 20–30 years to pay for that.

So, are there any glimmers of hope? I am sorry to say it is quite hard to discern any right now. The inevitability of the economic cycle means that growth will eventually return. Realistically, it may take more than ten years from the lowest point of the cycle for the economy to get back to a normal growth pattern – and global signs of growth are a little mixed at the moment. Add in big demographic changes within our own population and big shifts in migration patterns, and you can see how the future has uncertainty written all over it. The New Public Sector is a near certainty, so best get used to it.

But great news: the sensible public sector manager will want to prepare the best way they can. Luckily, you have taken an early step by reading *How to Survive Austerity*!

There are many opportunities to be more efficient, to look for synergies between services and groups of people, to streamline activity, not least through greater use of electronic means and investment in systems, processes and facilities. We have also seen many examples of local authorities sharing chief executives, police services sharing both back-office functions and rarely used high-end equipment as well as NHS organisations coming together to streamline patient experience.

We see more joining up being mandated in the NHS in England, with a five-year plan that sets out a number of improvement initiatives. In Scotland, we have seen the Community Empowerment Act help to empower community bodies through the ownership of land and buildings, and to strengthen their voices in the decisions that matter to them. And we have seen local authorities tackling their local agendas in 'Northern Powerhouse' areas by agreeing to combine functions in exchange for additional funding.

What can I do about it (and why should I care)?

I am assuming that, as a public sector manager of some influence, it will not be in your nature to do nothing. With your commitment to public service, you are unlikely to be prepared to stand idly by while your service is under threat. So I am proposing a sensible methodology – CHERISH – to guide you in establishing the value of your service and presenting it to others.

There cannot be any guarantee of success, but even if you do not achieve all of your aims, there are still benefits to be reaped from having made the effort. We will aim to satisfy the three areas our benchmark respondents identified. To refresh your memory, these were:

- To simplify the message we give to the public on what services we deliver and why.
- To be really clear about how much our service costs.
- To explain clearly what comparisons we have done to persuade people we are offering the best value for money.

The public sector has often made very simple ideas appear very complex to the layperson. Initiatives the private sector pick up and deliver very quickly often seem to take years to put into practice in the public sector. And as you can see from this chapter, time is not on your side.

The good news is that you do not need to wait until your Chief Executive or Divisional Director or Operational Board (delete as appropriate) decides to change your organisation. While all organisations need to exert control and plan change, piloting is something that can be applied quickly and is one way to start delivering change now. Identifying a methodology that is simple and has few overheads could be one way forward.

So CHERISH is something you can start tomorrow, setting yourself a goal for two or three months' time. It will have to be a light-touch project (administratively), because, to be honest, you have not got two years.

The downside to this is, not surprisingly, that chief executives etc. may not want all their managers going off and doing this. This is where your ability to present your ideas and your service persuasively is vitally important. You must be an evangelist for your service. We will explore how you achieve that in the coming chapters.

What other options are open to me?

The conventional wisdom used to be that once the economy recovers, opportunities in the private sector open up for those who have left the public sector. At the same time, the whole economy grows and the public sector grows again, creating more opportunity. Can we be sure this cycle will recur in future?

A 2011 survey conducted by Barclays Corporate and the FT found that 57% of private sector employers surveyed said they were not interested in hiring ex-civil servants, largely because they do not think they have the right skills to flourish in the private sector. The picture may have changed since then and 43% do not share that view. But the future will be typified by tighter competition for *all* jobs, so everyone should be maximising their skills and improving their marketability both within and outside the public sector.

So I would end this chapter by asserting you have nothing to lose by taking up the challenge of championing your service, and everything to gain. Even if you cannot save your service, the skills and experience you acquire in the attempt will maximise your future success.

We are at the start of the journey to the New Public Sector. You are taking the first steps to ensure you understand what will be demanded of you. You are in a great place to emerge as one of the leaders in that new landscape.

So now let us get on with doing what you are best at: delivering the best public services you can.

CHAPTER 3

The Seven Steps To Becoming Cherished

What this chapter covers

- It provides a guide to help you clarify what your services really deliver and explains to you why you must be able to define this in under a minute.
- It outlines a step-by-step process that will help you make your services CHERISHed, which in turn will allow the public and the government to recognise your value.
- It follows through with advice on what you should do once you have made your services CHERISHed to improve further and help others do the same.

How do I maximise my chances of surviving?

CHERISH is not a single methodology or formula, as is often the way with strategic solutions and those implemented by large consultancies. CHERISH is also not rocket science. It is a collection of tips, techniques and questions spun into an easy-to-follow framework that you can deploy in a way that is appropriate to your circumstances and your service.

I would be very surprised if you do not already possess the skills and experience you need to deliver the required outcomes, as you are managing a public service. What you do need to do is to hone those skills and develop your own innovative approach to presenting your service, your costs and your performance clearly – and to gather evidence to make a persuasive 'pitch' to the public and those at the top of your organisation.

The pitch is a key activity and this area is where most managers need development. The first step to becoming a CHERISHed service is to develop clarity on what you do and how much your service costs, and then to explain in simple terms why you offer value for money.

You will need to do this both internally and externally, to your internal sponsors (like chief executives, etc.) as well as to wider stakeholders and the public. You must be brave and confident in telling people what you do and how much you cost. You have to make them all care. You have to convince them your service is worth supporting. And you want them to CHERISH your service.

Citizen engagement

I worked with a rural local authority several years back that pioneered citizen engagement long before it was fashionable. Councillors of all parties signed up to a commitment to explain the services delivered to local people and employed local and sector-specific advocates to help them do this. The local population loved it and became fierce defenders of their local services when they came under pressure from central government.

If none of the things I mentioned above sound earth-shattering, then that is good news. Hopefully most people reading this book will already be doing those things. But the way CHERISH works will challenge you to go further and refine those messages, to condense them to the point where you and your staff can all deliver an 'elevator pitch' for your service.

That is a term much loved in the USA. Think Richard Branson, Duncan Bannatyne, or Deborah Meaden. Richard/Duncan/Deborah gets into your lift (all three of them together is probably beyond most people, so do not worry!) and they push the button for the 20th floor. You want them to invest in your business or your idea. You now have about 45 seconds tops to make a connection, get your story out and give them your card.

Sounds very un-public sector? We generally all only have 45 seconds these days to listen to other people's pitches and decide if we care or not. So why should your public be any different? The next sections of *How to Survive Austerity* set out the steps to enable you to do this, and more, for your service. That is how you maximise your chances of surviving.

How to use this framework

In the previous chapter, we explored why you should aim to improve your service, and why making incremental improvements will probably not cut it in the coming years. The demands of the New Public Sector will require you to make the public CHERISH your service.

It starts with ensuring you can offer a clear message about your service and it ends with you helping others to achieve the same thing once you have set your service on the path to continuous improvement. But what does making the public CHERISH your service actually mean?

Well, one definition of CHERISH is to 'hold something dear or to protect and care for someone lovingly'. Now while actually expecting people to love public services maybe asking a little too much, we all understand the passion and call to action we feel when something dear to us is placed under threat. We have a protective instinct that motivates us to fight for what we believe to be right.

So your aim is to use this simple seven-step approach to motivate the public you serve to stand up and fight for your service. I introduced the seven steps that comprise the CHERISH process in the previous chapter. We will go through each of the seven steps in turn and explore what you need to do, how you know you have been successful and what to do next.

I refer throughout *How to Survive Austerity* to documents and tools designed to help you deliver change. I have made those documents available to you at www.newpublicsector.com. There you will find additional resources, articles and the experiences of others who have been on this journey, and you can share these with your colleagues and stakeholders. There are also offers of help, support and challenge from others to get you started quickly.

CHERISH PRE-PLANNING

Here is a simple four-stage process diagram to help you frame your thinking and gather together your ideas. A description of suggested first actions for each of the four pre-planning steps is provided below.

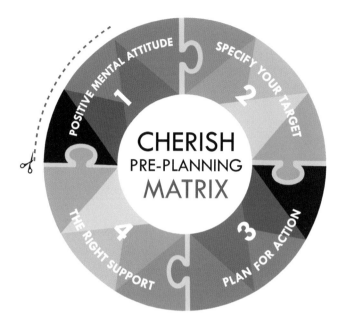

FIGURE 6: CHERISH pre-planning matrix

Positive mental attitude

First things first. Do you want to deliver the outcomes we talked about at the start of *How to Survive Austerity*? Are you brave? Do you want to give this austerity thing a poke in the eye? Yes? Great, that's a good start. That positive mental attitude – and backbone – is just the thing you will need to help you steer your course over the next three months or so. Not quite as self-assured and a bit of self-doubt? That's OK; as long as you share the desire to succeed and willingness to try, then you are still in the right place. You will need to keep your eye on the vision and on your aim throughout this process as well as doing the day job. Not easy, I know, but keep this in your mind and we are off to a good start.

Next, decide what you are going to seek to improve and make CHER-ISHed.

Identify your target

The key to being able to move quickly and effectively is to identify a very specific service project with very clear benefits and to develop a practical improvement plan. Having a structured approach to delivering projects and programmes so that they are aligned with your organisation's strategic and operational plans is critical. I recently came across the Business Lifesystem®, which is an example of such an approach. It uses the concept of Delivery Management Vehicles (DMVs) to ensure projects deliver the capability, transformational change and benefits required by your business strategy. It offers a better alternative to the usual project and programme management techniques; you can decide if this approach is for you by looking at the Business Lifesystem® approach at www.businesslifesystem.com. Make sure what you have in mind is achievable over a short time frame. This is not going to be a big-bang restructure that will absorb half your management resources for the next six months. Remember, CHERISH need not be a one-off. Having completed one project successfully, you could look to another area of activity, or you could refine the process on the basis of your experiences first time round. Or perhaps you will, on the basis of your achievement, see a way forward for larger-scale change. Austerity brings opportunities as well as dangers.

Plan for action

I have already said that time is of the essence. Austerity is banging on your door, so you need to do something about this now – easier said than done in the public sector, where lead times tend to be measured in many months, even if you are lucky. My challenge to you is to set yourself a twelve-week target for action.

Your initial aim is to be able to define your service in terms of outcomes, costs and value to the legendary 'man on the Clapham omnibus' in less than 30 seconds. For those of you who don't know who that man is, Wikipedia provides us with the following description: 'The man on the Clapham omnibus is a hypothetical reasonable person, used by the courts in English law, where it is necessary to decide whether a party has acted as a reasonable person would – for example, in a civil action for negligence. The man on the Clapham omnibus is a reasonably educated and intelligent but nondescript person, against whom the defendant's conduct can be measured. The term was introduced into English law during the Victorian era, and is still an important concept in British law.' This all means that while you may know your service inside out you need to be able to present that service and what it offers persuasively to that man on the Clapham omnibus.

The right support

If you try to do this in a vacuum, the outcome will not be well received. You will need the permission of an appropriate sponsor within your organisation. It may be the chief executive, it could be your service director, or your regional director or your chief superintendent, etc. With an appropriate sponsor, there is a better chance that once you have worked through this process successfully, you will be able to spread this technique to other services in their sphere of operation and to colleagues, and wider changes will inevitably require corporate support to implement. And there will come a point when you will want to engage your staff in the CHERISH process, with those staff becoming advocates for your service. They will be instrumental at the 'Share' stage as well as playing a key role throughout the project. I recommend identifying CHERISH Champions to work with you so that the process is done *with* staff, not *to* them.

So use these four steps as your pre-commencement tick box. You will also find lots of useful tools and checklists at www.newpublicsector.com to help you start your journey. I have suggested a timescale of 12 weeks to complete each CHERISH project. This is, of course, indicative but doable. Below I have prepared a sample, and very much outline, timetable you can use to plan your own actions. You will need to modify this plan to meet your own requirements but this will serve as a good starting point for you.

WEEK	STAGE
0	Pre-Planning
1-4	Clarity
2-5	How Much?
3-6	Evaluate
6-10	Reportage
11+	Improve
12+	Share
12+	Help

FIGURE 7: Outline CHERISH Timetable

Section 1: CLARITY

What does 'clarity' mean?

In order to get anyone to care genuinely about your service you have to tell them first of all what 'it' is, and then why he or she should value 'it'.

I mentioned earlier about you and your staff developing an 'elevator pitch' for your service. I suggested that we all generally only spend 45 seconds listening to other people's pitches these days and deciding if we want to care or not. In today's busy world, most people do not have long to engage with things they are not already connected to. As a manager in the New Public Sector, if you are not connecting to people then your service is not going to be around very long.

Take a look back at *Figure 5, the Emerging Model of the New Public Sector* I used to summarise the New Public Sector. Notice how the diagram highlights the importance of engaging the public in a way that has not been required in the past. You need to involve them and make them care. So I would argue you must learn to engage with people in a new way. You have to learn to deliver that elevator pitch for your service in 45 seconds, then reduce it to 30 seconds, then to 20 seconds. In that time, you need to get across to your listener exactly what your service does, who you do it for and why they should care about your service. In the New Public Sector, the challenge is to be succinct about the changes you propose and the potential benefits to the listener.

I came across a great book written by the entrepreneur and author Daniel Priestley, called *Key Person of Influence* (www.keypersonofin-fluence.com/kpi-method). Daniel's book provides some great insights into the development of a perfect pitch. In his book, he tells us how he often asks business people to rate themselves on how well they think they answer the question 'what do you do?' Most give themselves seven or eight out of ten. Daniel asks readers to consider that, 'If everyone you meet knows over 250 people, scoring a ten out of ten would mean they want to tell everyone about you. A ten out of ten could mean people might update their Facebook status about you'. Perhaps this could include providing positive comment about your service and maybe even defending your service if it was under attack.

How would you rate your current 'pitching skills'? How would you rate those of your staff? Do you have a message the public understands about what you deliver? Do you even have a message your own organisation understands? If you undertook a random poll in the street and asked about how your service is delivered, what answers would you expect back? If you do not have a clear message, how do you expect people to care about your service? Having a clear message about what you do, what you deliver and why people should care is essential for remaining part of the New Public Sector.

There is also a firm line to be drawn between having a clear message about what you do and 'spin'. This latter term has fallen into much disrepute after spin got a little out of hand a few years ago. If you consider for one moment blurring the clarity of your message and being less than honest and direct, most people will spot that spin a mile off.

So you need to be straight with people. Remember that most people you engage will want to believe you. After all, most of them will believe that they, personally, are 'footing the bill' for your service, so you need to be clear-sighted about what you deliver and how much it costs.

What do I need to do?

It's all about the pitch

Imagine the Coliseum in Ancient Rome, filled with a frenzied crowd. And imagine the Emperor seeking some direction from the spectators before he gives a 'thumbs up/thumbs down' to the gladiator before him. The common assumption is that 'thumbs down' means the gladiator must perish. Leaving aside the historical accuracy of that assumption, you want to achieve the opposite of that – you want 'thumbs up' and to be CHERISHed.

Visualise for a moment your service as a gladiator fighting other services for survival in the 'Arena of Austerity'. Your aim is to get a positive response from those judging you – perhaps judging you against other services. And rather than use hard weaponry (tempting though that may appear at times), your prime tools are the powers of persuasion. Key in your armoury is a perfect pitch that you can deliver clearly and confidently at will. You need to attain clarity in your offer, to borrow a phrase from the commercial sector.

So even if that sounds quite un-public sector, you need to develop a series of pitches you can deliver to suit the different circumstances and situations you face as a public sector manager. You are not going to arrive at that perfect pitch by locking yourself away in a darkened room. The pitch has to be something that you have lived, breathed, practised and honed – and that emerges as something you truly believe.

Daniel Priestley's book, *Key Person of Influence*, describes how to arrive at such a pitch: 'This means you need to write out a presentation pitch, learn it and practise it until you own it. You know you have it when you can talk passionately about your topic for three minutes or three hours without much preparation. Getting to this point requires you to start with some structure.'

So, like a gladiator, you must spend time honing your craft. You have a vital message to communicate, but to perfect it you must test it continually, and test it with as many people as you can in as many situations as you can. In this section, we identify the steps you need to take to develop your pitch and what content must go into it. I outline techniques that will help you develop your pitch and test it before it goes out to the public. That will only be done at the Reportage stage of CHERISH; you stop short of taking your pitch outside your organisation at this stage.

Be yourself

A few years ago, a Cabinet Minister with a strong regional accent underwent voice training to appear 'less regional' in different parts of the country. The individual was clearly uncomfortable with this new form of diction and appeared both wooden and false. This showed through in many media appearances and, as a result, the public lost belief in the message and some parts of the press used it as leverage against the Minister in question.

There are many ways to structure a short pitch to grab the attention of people and engage them. The overall aim is to present yourself as being both clear and credible. You must establish quickly why your audience should consider you are worth listening to. Remember, you do not have long to grab the imagination and interest of your audience.

- First, you must outline clearly the service you are responsible for and what it delivers – perhaps you can provide an example of what would happen if your service were not delivered.
- Second, you must provide the audience with an idea of how much is being delivered, to whom, when and where. Provide some examples of what that means in terms of things delivered per capita, per householder, per user, etc.
- Next, you must persuade the audience that you offer the best way to deliver this service and that there are no alternatives today that could deliver the service better.
- Finally, you must provide some proof of what you have told people and clearly substantiate your claim to offer the best service delivery by perhaps citing improvements you have made, benchmarking your service against those of your peers or alternatives, and perhaps providing a case study or live example that adds weight to what you are saying.

Once you have completed your pitch, you must ask your audience for their approval and acceptance that the service you describe represents the best there is. We will return to a number of methodologies and channels for delivering your message in later sections of this chapter. But your pitch must stand on its own and motivate people to CHERISH your service.

When you do this at the Reportage stage, you will have all the information the public will need to make a decision to CHERISH your service. I do recognise seeking approval in this way could be a tall order when we are talking about public services that people often take for granted, or often do not want to be delivered (such as collecting income tax or perhaps implementing resourcing decisions). But you must aim to capture the approval of your audience in sufficient numbers to enable you to demonstrate that you have presented your service clearly to your audience and that they have understood that service.

I also acknowledge at this early stage that there are many parts of the public sector that do not directly engage with the public, such as internal providers of services to their organisation. I am thinking here about services such as HR, IT, accounting and other support services – all essential parts of making public sector services work but with clients that are almost certainly internal. Such services can also benefit from CHERISH, although the references made to engaging the public will need to be interpreted in terms of your own service and clients. The lessons and approach proposed under CHERISH are no less applicable, but you will need to find ways to make the application relevant to your own internal clients. You could even offer support as one of the key supplier stakeholders of public-facing services. So throughout *How to Survive Austerity*, the references to services engaging with the public apply to you equally.

You can use the broad structure highlighted above to prepare a pitch for your own service. You will need to draft, redraft and draft again. Refine and finalise your pitch and then practise it over and over again. Remember, it cannot be a great pitch if it only exists in your head. Remember the lift I referred to earlier? You could just smile at your fellow traveller, but they will only act if you have engaged them effectively.

Some typical questions you will want to ask yourself when you are putting your pitch together might include:

- What does my service deliver, who does it deliver it to, why is it delivered and what would happen if it stopped being delivered?
- Can the service be delivered in a better or different way, could it be combined with another service to deliver more, could some element of it be changed so it delivers better outcomes?
- How many outcomes/interventions/things does your service deliver annually/monthly/weekly/daily?
- Where is it delivered, why is it delivered there and could it be delivered from different locations?
- How is it delivered, who helps you deliver the outcomes, who pays for the service and why is it organised in the way it is?

Be specific and avoid the use of any jargon or 'organisation-speak'. Remember that man on the Clapham omnibus. What would he understand in your use of language? I have put some useful tools, downloads and links on www.newpublicsector.com that may help you in your thinking, and there are great sources of support available to help you frame your argument and develop a great pitch. This is only a guide, so you will need to think about how this would work for your service. Public services are as varied in what they deliver as are the delivery organisations themselves.

It could be that at first your pitch is a little too structured. You will need to practise delivering your pitch to your own staff and stakeholders and then refining it on the basis of their responses. With rehearsal and refinement will come clarity.

Own your message

Modern media has highlighted the need for public figures to appear to be not only confident in the delivery of their message, but also to be word perfect. Almost all media-savvy politicians use technology, such as auto-cue screens that are near-invisible to their audience, to help them deliver their message, but the really memorable speeches in recent years have come from politicians who have spoken from the heart, having rehearsed their message over and over ahead of its delivery.

You need to move away from any suggestion that your pitch is 'scripted'. You need the confidence to talk about your service spontaneously, otherwise people will not believe you are being sincere. Think about how actors on stage or in films persuade us they are something they are not, because they have completely internalised their script. If your pitch sounds too rehearsed, you probably have not rehearsed it enough.

A final quote from Daniel Priestley's book sums up exactly what you are trying to achieve. 'One of our clients taught his 50+ team how to pitch properly. Everyone, from the receptionist to the directors, had to know the three-minute pitch by heart. The results were stunning: the entire company saw greater alignment, more energy, more innovation and more sales, which could all be tracked back to this pitching activity.'

So think about how your pitch will be delivered by people other than yourself. If your pitch fails to convince whenever it is delivered, then it will impact on everything else you deliver, so make sure you tailor the message for different audiences and for the different people delivering it.

The continual feedback from your sponsors and stakeholders will also allow you to improve and refine your message. Only when your 'sword can be burnished no more' (meaning your pitch can be improved no further), will you be ready to present it to the most demanding audience of all – the public.

Engaging others

You may decide to develop a pitch about your whole service or only part of it. You must be clear on what you are pitching or you will not achieve that required clarity. Once you have decided which service, part service or activity you will focus on, you must summarise this in your pitch. You must think about how you are going to get your message out and what would constitute success in terms of connection with the public. One hundred people providing positive feedback? One thousand? One million? The answer must reflect your circumstances and your service. But defining success at the start is something you must consider. Think also about the ways you can evidence that success.

You must ensure your message is a single, clear and consistent message, particularly if you have a series of pitches that will be delivered in different circumstances. The core message must be consistent but tailored to suit each engagement group. Avoid at all costs having different content for different people.

Engagement is a continuum and you need to build it as you go. The diagram below provides some suggestions on how to build your engagement support.

FIGURE 8: Levels of engagement support

Start at the bottom with some of the people in your 'peers and family' group. These are the people you should already be engaged with, and with whom you can communicate most easily. These people could be your peers, other managers, and other services in the same organisation. Using the relative security of this group, try out your pitch and seek feedback. It may prove to be embarrassing at first, but you will soon overcome this with practice and your confidence will grow. Then consider extending your reach beyond that to your professional network, and perhaps even to your family, who should be able to support you in your endeavour. And be warned, such groups often provide the most critical feedback, so do not be put off.

Once you have practised and you feel more confident about the clarity of your message, you can go a little further still, to what I have called your 'friendly stakeholders'. They might be partner organisations, people who work within your own service or organisation or possibly suppliers, but not at this stage the public or wider stakeholder groups. You will need to make your own decisions on who best fits into this group. Repeat the exercise of practising your pitch, receiving feedback and refining your message further. By now, you will be developing greater confidence and greater clarity in your message.

These two groups are where you will find your 'CHERISH Champions'. These are the people who can advocate on behalf of your service and whom you can use to test new material, feed back to you and refine pitch material. Your CHERISH Champions should be able to challenge you throughout the whole process and be able to provide feedback on your progress at each of the stages. Some individuals should be internal to your organisation and some external – it is useful to have a mix of the two. Your external Champions are likely to have a more detached perspective that will help you to spot 'elephant traps' and they should not be afraid to tell you about them.

The next level of engagement support is provided by 'neutral stakeholders'. In this group I suggest you include more distant stakeholders such as suppliers, third-sector groups and others you work with perhaps on a less regular or frequent basis. At this stage, you may also want to reaffirm that you are working within your organisational or corporate standards and guidelines on engagement. But at the same time, ensure your CHERISH timetable does not become bogged down or delayed. I will leave it to you to decide how best you can achieve this as there is much variation in such standards.

And then at the very top of the pyramid, we find the most important people: the public. This is the most important group and probably the group that will, at the Reportage stage, judge you most harshly.

The whole CHERISH process focuses on you getting your message across to this group so that they understand your service and the value it brings to their lives.

We are not talking here about a public consultation; that has a very formal meaning in some parts of the public sector. What we are talking about is engaging the public in a far more direct and focused way. And for internal-facing service managers, the message is to engage with your clients so they know they are receiving the best possible service and one they understand and value. So before you approach the top-level group in the pyramid, whether they be the public or internal clients, you must finish your pitch, complete your review of costs and delivery arrangements (Stage 2, How Much?) and complete an assessment of alternatives to allow the public and clients fair comparison (Stage 3, Evaluate).

This section has concentrated on you being clear about what you offer. The next two sections will focus on adding additional cost and comparison information to that clear message. By the time you approach the top level of your engagement pyramid, you must have completed and sharpened that message and have a succinct and arresting proposition the public and clients will want to hear and engage with.

Remember that when it comes to engaging with the public, you will have to go to them. You cannot expect the public to come to you just because you would like them to. It is a good idea to look out for opportunities that provide a ready-made 'platform' for presenting your pitch. Such opportunities will vary according to the sector and area you are working in, but think about public forums that are held regularly, perhaps third-sector engagement events and meetings, local neighbourhood meetings, Citizen's Advice Bureau sessions, and corporate 'meet the public' and stakeholder events – in fact, all the sorts of occasions that might provide you with access to the people you want to involve. So start thinking about this now as it will be of use to you at the Reportage stage.

You may also want to develop a stakeholder map for your project. I have provided a couple of examples and some links that may be useful as part of the online resources at www.newpublicsector.com.

When you engage with the public you will need to listen hard to the responses you receive. A polite or neutral response is the worst thing you can get when you tell people what your service delivers. Polite responses will take you nowhere. You ideally need people to ask questions of you, to be sufficiently engaged and interested to ask more. You need to hook people into what you do and deliver.

Once people are hooked by what you deliver, they should want more. Your goal is to make them want more information about what you do and what you have achieved, so that by the time you have developed the version of your pitch you will deliver to the public, you will have already thought about the questions they could ask you and the answers you will give.

The next two sections provide more advice on the quantitative and comparison aspects of those questions, so that when you are asked 'how much does that service cost?' or 'is there a better way you could deliver that service?' you will have worked through the issues and have clear responses to those and many other questions.

Only when you have these issues clear in your head will you actually be ready to face the public. Ideally, you will have a scheduled time to deliver a 'presentation pitch'. This could range from a few minutes to a few hours, depending on the circumstances. A presentation pitch cannot be left to chance. When you have a captive audience you must be prepared to cover all your bases. You also cannot sound ill-prepared. You must know your pitch so well that it comes from your heart rather than your memory.

How will I know If I have got there?

There is no simple answer to this question and only you can decide. However, there are a number of indicators we can use to judge if you have done sufficient work on your pitch to move on to the next stage in the CHERISH process. Here are my suggested indicators and of course you can always extend this checklist, perhaps enlisting the help of your CHERISH Champions, who will be able to challenge and test you. My top indicators are:

1. You will be happy to deliver your pitch in any given situation and will be confident in your delivery.
2. Those in your engagement network will tell you they are happy.
3. You can deliver your pitch without a script and without hesitation in work as well as in social situations.
4. You will begin to visualise yourself delivering your pitch to the public.
5. Peers in your organisation will notice a difference in the way you present and speak about your service.
6. You will begin to think about completing the process for your service and about ways you can help other services achieve the same clarity.

Section 2: HOW MUCH?

What does 'how much' mean?

The title of this section says it all, really. You need to calculate an accurate cost for providing your service and express it in a way that is meaningful to a reasonable man – remember the one on the Clapham omnibus?

That overall cost should include the cost of all resources, goods, other services, expenses and support that contribute to the delivery of your service. And then you need to find ways to reduce that cost to the lowest level possible. You will use that cost during the next stage of CHERISH, comparing it with the cost of any alternatives that may exist, in order to persuade the public you are offering good value.

As a manager within the public sector, you will, I am sure, already have a really good picture of the costs of your own service. You will have an annual budget and I am sure you monitor your expenditure against that budget regularly. You will also have a clear picture of what organisational costs are added to your direct service costs. I am thinking here of things like IT costs, central management and professional costs, as well as strategic costs and overheads.

The extent to which organisations devolve and monitor those costs at individual service level varies enormously. Some public sector organisations have delegated budgets down to service level; others are content to have service level costs monitored by individual managers but leave organisational and structural costs unallocated.

For the purposes of CHERISH, you need to make great efforts to understand all the costs that make up your overall cost. When you take your pitch to the public, they will expect you to be open and honest with them about both what you do and how much that costs. If you are not clear about both of those things or you are not confident that your costs are accurate, people will be right to question why they should listen to you and, consequently, whether they should care about your service.

What do I need to do?

CHERISH is a two-way street that relies on you and the public trusting each other and being honest with each other. For some public sector organisations, such openness may prove to be difficult at first. Many organisations may not want their managers to question the overall organisational or structural costs. They may also not want their managers to share that information with the public. But the demands of the New Public Sector will mean that such views must change. We are facing expectations on the part of the public for much greater understanding of what they are paying for, and government, in its turn, will question costs that do not demonstrably and directly contribute to the delivery of service outcomes.

So this section is all about developing clarity of understanding about your costs, reducing them once you have a true picture of them, and encouraging your organisation to be more transparent about those costs.

For many public sector managers, the scale of the cuts they need to make to their existing service costs will depend on what austerity targets have been determined by their top-level funding body. We identified earlier that the extent of exposure to austerity currently depends largely on where you are in the public sector landscape and/or where you are in the UK. Different factors will come into play in different parts of the public sector.

The New Public Sector has a key objective of doing more for less that provides a clear focus for your efforts and actions. If there is a general trend for a spending reduction of 20% in your part of the public sector, there seems little point in spending time drawing up a plan to reduce your costs by 5%. The extent of austerity means you are unlikely to be able to offer incremental improvement in your service and cost reduction plans. In the emerging shape of the New Public Sector, your cost reduction options are more likely to look like this:

- 10%–15% annual savings?: 'You should be doing this anyway!'
- 15%-25% annual savings?: 'Your pips should be starting to squeak!'
- 25%+ annual savings: 'Now you understand what the New Public Sector is all about!'

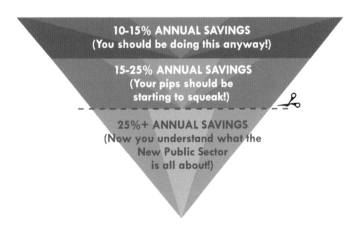

FIGURE 9: Cost Reduction Considerations Framework

Different parts of the UK's public sector are moving at a different pace on that savings journey, so if you have been preparing contingency cost reduction plans over the past few years, now is the time to start dusting them off.

The first thing you need to do is to understand your current costs and what you deliver for those costs.

Most public sector managers will already have clarity on those costs and will know how many outcomes they deliver for that cost. There are many variants of performance monitoring frameworks covering cost assessments in use in the public sector. It is not my intention to add any more. CHERISH will rely on you to identify what is used in your own organisation, and what works best for your service, to enable you populate that framework accordingly.

The cost framework you choose should provide you with a means of identifying your costs and supporting your understanding of the impact any reduction has on your bottom line. This will give you the clarity your project needs. Ensure the data you use is accurate, up to date, and appropriately linked to other review activity your organisation may undertake. You cannot undertake your exercise in a vacuum when other services may be reviewing what they are doing and how much they cost. As a minimum, your framework should enable you to understand your costs under the following headings and allow you to drill down so you can properly understand where they come from.

Cost Heading	Description
Direct service costs	Costs that are directly attributable to your service such as staffing costs, costs directly associated with delivering your service, and costs arising from bought-in services that directly contribute to the delivery of your service.
Indirect service costs	Costs that are not directly chargeable to the delivery cost of your service and may have fixed or variable elements to them. Examples may include non-service-specific administration, personnel and security costs.
Departmental, organisational or management costs	Each organisation allocates their nonservice-specific costs in a different way and there is a significant industry that supports allocation methods. Such costs are often described as overheads, management overheads, or organisational costs, so you will need to make sure you properly understand how your organisation allocates such costs to your particular service.
Other costs	Some organisations will also have financing charges that are allocated to each service or business unit, such as a share of PFI costs, transformation costs and other asset-related costs. Again, you will need to make sure you properly understand how your organisation allocates such costs to your particular service.
Annual deliverables	This is what you deliver annually for the costs listed above. You need to make sure you understand why any significant variations in annual volumes have occurred and what impact such variations have had on your costs. Above all, you need to align the question of 'how many' with 'what', identifying a unit cost where possible, and making sure both sides of the equation are compatible and will be understandable to the public.

FIGURE 10: Minimum data for service costing framework

61

If your existing organisational cost framework falls short of having this level of data, you may need to seek information from your organisation to allow you to gather this. The level of information noted on the previous page is not unreasonable and will be the type of information the public will want. It would also not be unreasonable for them to consider gaps or uncertainties as an attempt to be less than transparent, so this is something your organisation will need to consider sooner rather than later anyway.

As regards your deliverables, most public sector managers can clearly articulate *what they deliver* in quantitative terms. In some cases, that clarity may fall short of what the public want, but the 'Clarity' stage of CHERISH should have addressed that. Equally, the outputs and deliverables of some services may be more difficult to describe than those of others for a number of reasons. For example, the service may have multiple outcomes, all of which are of equal importance; or it may have mixed caseloads; or perhaps variability in the time cases take to complete – all of which may result in difficulties in defining a single, understandable outcome.

This is something you will need to work on with your CHERISH Champions when you are crafting your pitch. Describing clearly what you do is a prerequisite for describing how much it costs and how much/many you deliver. You may need to refine the 'cost and quantity' message as much as you refine the 'what' message, so do not worry if you cannot do this immediately. At least if your costs are known, you can respond better to the question 'what do I get for my money?' when asked.

Whatever you decide to include or exclude, you have got to be honest about having done so. You need to state clearly if a cost has been excluded and why, or whether outcomes have been combined to reflect a 'basket of outcomes'. If you do not include all relevant costs, for example, perhaps not revealing IT, accounting or management costs, you are not likely to be able to offer accurate comparisons with alternative service providers, and you are unlikely to be able to convince the public if you stumble over the accuracy of your data.

Do also bear in mind that the public sector is able to draw on a certain amount of goodwill, and community and social input. The cost of some of that support may well be zero but the value significant, for example, the input provided by many community, third- and fourth-sector enterprises and groups. Such support can be legitimately mentioned in the cost analysis even if there are no costs associated with it. This could be used in later comparisons as an offset against alternative service provision offered, for example, by the private sector, who could offer economies of scale, corporate relationships and perhaps branding, but might not be building social capital as they do so. But as a rule of thumb, if your service is not currently paying for something, you should not put it in as a cost.

The third-sector dimension

I worked with a London local authority to develop a pan-service third-sector strategy that sought to identify just how much funding was coming into the area through third-sector organisations. The startling conclusion was that services to the value of some £2 billion per annum were being delivered by local and national third-sector organisations to the same clients the local authority was supporting. The implementation of the strategy identified a number of projects receiving duplicate funding and prevented significant overlaps in service delivery.

This approach is intended to offer a 'light touch' means of improving public sector efficiency. It is also intended to be an exercise in applying common sense and appropriate levels of external challenge. It is not intended to spawn an industry, as was the case back in the 1990s, when many local authorities up and down the country expended a lot of effort proving there was no competition requirement for various services under the Compulsory Competitive Tendering regime that was prevalent at the time. That generated a whole set of accountants proving there was no need for competition and another set proving there was. I do not recall a lot of actual service improvement emerging from the involvement of so many accountants.

Your calculations and estimates must be genuine, accurate and simple. This is all part of improving clarity, which is fundamental to the New Public Sector, and being able to get that information across to people. Having clarity on the 'what?' and the 'how much?' for your service and why it matters is the first step of this journey.

Reviewing current costs

Once you are happy that you have a cost framework that allows you to reflect your current costs and delivery arrangements accurately, you need to undertake some hard work to identify improvements and/or cost reductions. The New Public Sector demands that savings are made alongside finding more efficient ways of doing things. In some instances, the austerity agenda will demand that some services cease altogether. You need to identify improvements in the way you deliver your service *and* reduce your costs. And as we discussed in earlier sections, improving productivity in the public sector has a very different meaning from improving productivity in the private sector.

I will mention only briefly the need to improve how you do things before focusing on the options for identifying cost reductions. There are some critical analysis questions you need to ask yourself, including:

- What is it we are doing?
- How do we do it?
- Is it needed?
- Are there efficiencies to be made?
- Can it be done by someone else?
- Is it more appropriate for it to be done by someone else?
- Could it be done in another way?
- Is there scope for technology to reduce the costs of the service in the long term?

I am sure this is something you are already likely to be doing as a normal part of your job. Your organisation will already have arrangements for reviewing service costs and delivery arrangements. You may want to consider using a tried-and-tested (some would say traditional) methodology called Method Study as one of the core processes you use to subject your service to systematic, critical scrutiny. Originally designed for the analysis and improvement of repetitive manual work, the approach has six steps, often shortened to SREDIM, as follows:

- Select (the work to be studied)
- Record (all relevant information about that work)
- Examine (the recorded information)
- Develop (an improved way of doing things)
- Install (the new method as standard practice)
- Maintain (the new standard proactively)

FIGURE 11: Method Study framework

You can find more details about its application at www.ims-productivity.com/page.cfm/content/Method-Study, including advice on how you can apply it to all types of activity at all levels of an organisation. There is an underlying simplicity to Method Study, but often simple is best. Once you have completed your review of current delivery arrangements and understand them fully, it is time to start doing some harder thinking.

Analysing efficiency

Method Study was used extensively in local authorities to examine the efficiency of direct and blue-collar services such as cleaning, refuse collection and vehicle maintenance. It was then extended more widely to white-collar activity such as administrative processes, and it sits at the core of Business Process Re-engineering. Many public sector bodies have used Method Study in combination with work measurement techniques to provide basic data about how long tasks take, how they are sequenced, and their relevance and value to the overall outcome.

What would happen if we stopped this service?

It may be worth making some time to watch a great programme shown on the BBC back in 2011, called *The Street That Cut Everything* (www.bbc.co.uk/programmes/b011crrw). Fronted by Nick Robinson, then the BBC's political editor, the programme persuaded 50 residents of a street in Preston to forgo all local authority services (excluding education and healthcare) for six weeks. The residents of the street were required to arrange alternative solutions and in exchange they received a 'rebate' of the council tax they would have paid over the six-week period.

The programme is worth watching if only to demonstrate how little people really know about the interconnectivity of their public services – and why we as managers need to consider those factors carefully before we act. During the experiment, refuse was no longer collected, street lighting was switched off and other services provided by the local authority were withdrawn. To make life more difficult the programme kindly arranged for the street to be daubed with graffiti, items to be fly-tipped, and even managed to find some spare dogs to foul the pavements. (The actors posing as anti-social teenagers alone make for compulsive viewing.)

The programme did, to be fair, receive its share of criticism for simplifying issues and portraying a somewhat contrived situation – but that is television. A more positive review was given by Archie Bland of *The Independent*, who wrote: "It is the first piece of popular television I've seen that grapples effectively with how such deep cuts will really play out." And that was back in 2011.

I cite this as a great example of the need to look out for unintended consequences and to explore the whole range of consequences flowing from your decisions before you make them. This extends to the very obvious impacts on user groups that would be a direct result of your decision, but also the wider ramifications for other services and other stakeholders.

The changes you have in mind may indeed make your service more efficient and cheaper, but do consider their social impact and the practical impact for direct as well as indirect stakeholders. For example, very obvious social impacts have arisen from the squeeze on the funding available for home visits to frail elderly people in some areas of the country. This is an area regularly cited as being at crisis point in the press and media. Some visits have ended up being so truncated that it has resulted in episodes of acute distress for these clients. Some parts of the public sector are now considering mandating the duration of visits and limiting the number of visiting staff in order to avoid confusion in the minds of clients.

Think about how reducing the number of environmental health inspections would save money, but it would be likely to result not only in poorer hygiene, leading to more outbreaks of food poisoning, and placing an additional burden on health services, but it might also lead to fewer opportunities to identify those working illegally or those claiming benefits while working.

Researching savings in commissioning costs

A Clinical Commissioning Group (CCG) reviewed spending on sterile supplies and equipment compared with similarly-sized CCGs across the country and found they were significantly above the average. The CCG identified all spending establishments in their area and approached a local university to source statistics students who might be interested in undertaking research on methods and systems used by other CCGs. The research revealed that the best-performing CCGs had combined their purchasing power with other CCGs as well as joining with public and private health sector buying consortia, dentists and clinics. The CCG reduced costs by almost 30% following rationalisation of what they purchased and the negotiation of a significant discount in return for a longer-term supply contract.

At the same time as you are seeking to reduce your costs, you will need to think about improving or at least maintaining your service levels. In the New Public Sector, the nature of those improvements is likely to be more 'joined up' than it has been in the past, so you will need to consider improvements that impact on the whole system, demonstrating the cohesiveness and interconnectivity of the public sector to the public.

By way of practical impacts, you need to consider the effect on internal and external supply arrangements and any consequences of breaking or altering the terms of contracts or supply. You will need to develop an understanding of what your own organisation wants to deliver and its appetite for real change. It is no good making £x in savings if you will end up having to pay back the same amount to disgruntled contractors. And bear in mind that some organisations will be keen to maintain the middle layers of their structure even if better arrangements can be devised. The New Public Sector is likely to bite hard within such organisations, and while some may be able to resist for a time, there is an inevitability that austerity will eventually force change.

Beware of making uninformed changes where services are already joined up in a cost-effective way. In restricting the availability of a Meals on Wheels service, for example, you might find that the third-sector organisation providing that service also has a contract to deliver books for the library service. If you stop the Meals on Wheels, it will cost twice as much to deliver the books. Become informed.

And while you are informing yourself about what can be reduced in your own service, you need to gather more understanding about connected services and their standards and performance indicators, and to familiarise yourself with their organisational sanctions and implications. In so doing, you become better informed about the place of your organisation in the bigger picture, and you make yourself more valued to the organisation.

Procurement savings in clinical support costs

A large university hospital NHS Trust employing almost 15,000 people provides a range of specialist services including heart, cancer, stroke, renal neurosurgery and major trauma. Using collaborative procurement has helped the Trust reduce risk for patients and staff and generate savings of around £650,000 per year on equipment such as infusion pumps and administration sets, film dressings, the introduction of safety needles in order to comply with legislation, and savings of more than £200,000 per year on aprons, gloves, surgical gloves, hearing aids, textiles and inks and toners.

In terms of options appraisal for identifying cost reductions and service improvements, there is a myriad of tools and techniques you can use to help you identify your best course of action. You are bound to have come across the simple SWOT (Strengths, Weaknesses, Opportunities and Threats) analysis, a useful basic tool for flushing out all issues. You may also have come across a framework using the 'PESTELO' headings; it is another good basic tool for populating your analysis by considering the issues at stake: Political, Economic, Social, Technological, Environmental, Legal, and Organisational. I have included examples of these as well as some newer techniques you can deploy at www.newpublicsector.com.

Keep it simple

As is the case throughout the application of CHERISH, simplicity is your watchword. Make sure you apply simple and well-tested techniques to identify, gather and collate all the information from your thinking. Remember you have given yourself a target of 12 weeks to get this project completed. Too often over the years, I have seen great industries grow up around developing innovative costing and improvement models, only for accountants to come back to first principles. Keep it simple.

Think about how much time you can really afford to spend in deliberating on financial models. Yes, you will need to spend sufficient time making sure you have included all the relevant information and in ensuring that that information is accurate. I would have thought this part of the CHERISH process should take no more than a couple of weeks, particularly, as I suspect, you will already have most of this information available to you and you are already well ahead in thinking about service improvements. This stage can also be undertaken concurrently with other tasks, so information gathering does not have to be the only thing going on.

Simple also means that it is perfectly fine to start off big. Start with broad headings for key budget areas. It is often difficult in some public sector organisations to get down to individual service areas and into a finer level of detail. Sometimes you will just have to make estimates, but if you do, be clear that you have done so and 'show your workings', as they used to say at school. Make plain the basis of your assumptions, so that you can be transparent with people at a later stage. Allowing up to two weeks for technical costing work will then leave you with a further two weeks for debating the minutiae. But as I mentioned above, work on other areas while this work is proceeding.

You can only base the CHERISH process on what is actually happening today. But you need to be alive to any seismic changes looming on the horizon and try to future-proof it as far as possible. Keep an eye on how the New Public Sector is emerging and changing – that will serve as a guide for your review work and the questions you need to ask of your service and your organisation. As a minimum, you must keep one eye on the future if only because we know that austerity is going to demand year-on-year improvements. And austerity, as we know, is not going to go away any time soon.

Generating innovation

Some years ago, I was involved in the New Local Government Network (http://www.nlgn.org.uk/), a think tank set up during 1997 to lead the reinvention of local government thinking. After slow initial uptake, the Network identified a number of major policy initiatives that were subsequently sponsored by government. The organisation has since gone on to lead the thinking and testing of new ways of doing things and today they describe their mission as 'to bring together the best in our sector to create a brighter future for local government'.

It would also be wise to remain aware of the financial health of other bodies who contribute to your service delivery, for example, suppliers, contractors and third-sector partners. Think about what alternatives there would be if you could no longer rely on them for supplies or services. We will return to this issue in later sections as a means of focusing on continuing the improvement process, but it is worth bearing in mind at this stage.

You will also need to think about how you can best test the workability and practicality of your improvements, such as developing formal risk assessments and scenario-testing frameworks. Such actions will allow any mobilisation or operational issues to be identified before you take your planned improvements to the public or to your clients. Inevitably, as with all change, there will be unanticipated issues that will arise and you will need to develop a series of 'Plan As' and 'Plan Bs' to suit the needs of your service. It is very likely that at least some of your proposed improvements and changes to the way you do things will involve an element of risk. Best to plan for these and to test each scenario to ensure you have an answer to the 'what if…' questions you will be asked.

The challenge is to draw all this work into one simple and consistent core message that you can tailor for different audiences and that will stand up to scrutiny from those different perspectives.

How will I Know when I have got there?

In terms of the information you are gathering, it is probably fair to say that you will recognise for yourself when you have got there. If you have been obliged to gather information in a fairly piecemeal way, when you slot in the last piece of information the calculations will make sense and your rationale will fall into place.

You will be personally happy about the level and quality of information you have to present to the public. You will be as confident as you can be that there are no questions you could not answer. You will have thoroughly reviewed the way your service works and properly scrutinised the costs that make up your service.

You will have available a transparent story about the data you have gathered, complemented by the formulae you have used in your calculations. You will be able to explain those formulae to the public, remembering that some things that appear obvious to insiders sometimes make no sense at all to those on the outside.

You will have all the information you need to populate your cost and output spreadsheet and you will be clear that you have all the contextual information about stakeholders, partners, suppliers etc. And you will have already tested your projections and will have built scenario testing into your plan to account for the things you can anticipate.

You may have even developed a checklist for yourself to help you be confident you have constructed a compelling case that will stand up well to external scrutiny and provide the basis for an effective pitch.

By the time you have done all this groundwork – the research, the hard thinking and the structuring of your project and crafting the messages about it – you will probably be so close to it that it will be difficult for you and for those most closely associated with it to get an objective view.

Now would be a great time to sound things out with your CHERISH Champions and your sponsor. Get them to challenge you, to question you and to test you. Do not blind them with too many options or their focus will be diluted in trying to distinguish between them. It might be enough simply to give them a couple of choices: to say 'we can do a basic service for £x, but for £y more, we could have the following add-ons', or to highlight where your challenge to the current ways of doing things has identified alternatives.

I doubt whether you will have got to the position of senior public sector manager without coming across a number of different techniques for generating 'critical friend'-type input into a project, but the list below provides just three examples. There are many more and you will need to pick one that works for you.

- Pinpoint: A formal facilitation package, initiated in Germany after World War II to establish reconstruction priorities, that is excellent at garnering views from all participants, scoring them and ordering them, and it can be tailored to the amount of time available. Even without the actual equipment, you can achieve a lot with large 'post-it' notes and inclusive, targeted questions.
- Edward de Bono's Six Hats Thinking: This could also be a useful tool, but you might want to adapt it slightly to, say, consider the reactions of different groups – stakeholders, users, contractors, suppliers – to your proposals.
- Reverse Thinking: What would you do if you wanted to have exactly the opposite effect from the one you are seeking? So you would ask yourself how you could make your service far more expensive and unappealing to those it is aimed at. It sounds ridiculous but it is a lot of fun for participants and often generates some rather telling points.

No matter which challenge method you use, one sign that you have 'got there' will be that you have offered up for challenge a proposition with enough clarity and sound financial and administrative common sense to enable your 'critical friends' to deliver a definitive answer, along with constructive suggestions for enhancements to the chosen proposal.

Once you are satisfied you have got to this point, you are ready to seek some external validation of your proposed costs and delivery arrangements. This will involve comparing and contrasting your offer with alternative supply arrangements.

Section 3: EVALUATE

What does 'evaluate' mean?

Once you have established clarity on *what* your service delivers and have identified how to reduce costs and optimise delivery arrangements, the next step is to understand how much people really value your service and to find out if they would value different delivery arrangements more.

The whole issue of value is a difficult one and never has Oscar Wilde's observation that cynics 'know the price of everything but the value of nothing' been truer. Who now is not cynical about the value of services delivered by public sector and private sector alike? You will need to work very hard to understand why people should value your service delivered in the way you are offering it. Remember that not all people you engage with will share your values. Recalling some of the comments in my opinion survey, not all people will value the public sector in the same way. The New Public Sector will demand that you demonstrate clearly that you have looked at all the options and have gained a mandate to become CHERISHed.

As part of taking your pitch to the public or to your internal clients, you will need to develop an understanding of what really motivates people when it comes to the type of service you are delivering. That could prove to be difficult, particularly if you are delivering public sector services that are not popular, but are necessary, such as council tax collection. You also will need to develop a good understanding of how your service compares with similar services, or services that deliver outcomes that can be compared to yours.

77

Collecting VAT

Many years ago, I was involved in the benchmarking of the costs of collecting many £billions of VAT payments. There were clearly no other organisations in the UK that did exactly this (HM Customs and Excise, as it was then, would have taken a somewhat dim view of that!) but we dug deeper into the processes that were being used at the time.

There were lots of processing delays adding to the cost, and once you factored in the large sums of money it became obvious that the comparison lay with large organisations who banked the many cheques they received through the post effectively. (The example predates electronic banking, which has delivered quantum leaps in efficiency, but it still demonstrates my point.)

Once the review team identified exemplar corporates who had honed their processes, the benchmarking of current and target costs was relatively easy.

Today, there are also many examples of commercial organisations delivering public services. After many years of outsourcing (and we will return to this later in this section), there are now many meaningful comparisons that can be made between different ways of doing things so you have little excuse for not seeking comparisons in service delivery that, hopefully, will support your assertion that your service offers good value.

Not doing such comparisons will simply lay you open to criticism that you have your own vested interests at heart. And while that may be true, if you can demonstrate you have done your homework and have factored best practice into your service, you stand a better chance of convincing the public or your clients that they should CHERISH your service.

What do I need to do?

You need to prove to yourself that the service delivery arrangements you are proposing, and the costs associated with that service delivery, are the best you can offer. You will need to be able to convince those you are pitching to that you have genuinely looked at alternatives and made efforts to improve the value you are delivering for their money.

How you do this depends very much on the part of the public sector you are working in. There will be many services that will be genuinely difficult to compare with any others, although there will always be at least some comparisons available for any activity. Often the best way to make this comparison is to find services that are offered in a different way, and to benchmark your own services against them. There are many sector-based benchmarking clubs in the public sector as well as in the wider non-public sector economy. There are also many parts of the public sector that use some form of 'league table', even if these are not formally published in some parts of the country.

There are public sector bodies that specialise in auditing and reviewing what constitutes best practice and best value. Many of these services can provide excellent sources of comparison information and it is worth engaging with them, as they are there to help you improve what you do. I have offered some links to such organisations at www.newpublicsector.com.

A key performance improvement technique that was introduced in the late 90s for local authorities was 'Best Value'. A replacement for the earlier Compulsory Competitive Tendering scheme, Best Value sought to balance considerations of price and quality alongside the notion of 'fitness for purpose'. The approach highlighted that while a 'Rolls-Royce' service might be a great aspiration (and perhaps limited parts of the public sector may still be able to justify this), a more economic 'mode of transport' was more appropriate – not the cheapest or cheap, just a service that offered a balance between cost and quality. The original application worked well and many services now offer more realistic service outcomes for more modest costs. The thinking behind the original concept is still a useful benchmark, although the New Public Sector may force a greater emphasis on lowering costs than has previously been the case.

Outsourcing of back-office functions has been the norm throughout the public service for many years. However, outsourcing has not been universally applied across the country and there are significant disparities in the application in, for example, local authorities in England compared to those in Scotland. The functions of the public sector in different parts of the country also differ dramatically depending on the tiers and structure of government. Where outsourcing has been applied, it has involved the contracting out of business processes to another organisation, often the private sector, but also increasingly third and fourth-sector organisations.

This practice often involves transferring employees, assets and other resources from the public sector to another body, although contractual relationships may take other forms. The public sector often views outsourcing as handing over control of public services to profit-making bodies, and consequently (particularly as far as staff are concerned) it is viewed as a threat. Yet the process is now well established within all parts of the public sector, and its growth is only likely to continue.

As a real test of Best Value, there can be little argument that a competitive tender between two or more commercial bodies leading to the award of a contract would appear to offer the best test. The public sector sets out its requirements and the market responds. The market price for delivering a given service is set by market suppliers and the balance of price and quality is set by the buyer. This will be correct at a given point, but commercial considerations may erode that equilibrium over time.

However, there is little better as a source of comparison information than the recent outturn of a competitive tendering exercise for a similar service. Even exercises undertaken some time ago provide some useful comparison. What's more, the delivery methodologies of commercial operations can often provide a great guide for the public sector manager.

Hybrid benchmarking

Some years ago, I was involved in the development of an approach we termed 'hybrid benchmarking', which was used in large central government departments to deliver efficiencies. Rather than undertake competitive tendering, my clients identified the likely market pricing and processes, and then sought to replicate those using internal bids. Run along similar lines to competitive tendering exercises, the practice was successful in delivering efficiencies averaging around 20% to 25%, which was, at the time, sufficient to yield the required efficiency savings.

There are also other delivery arrangements used within the public sector that can offer sources of comparison. These include formal and informal partnerships, joint ventures, as well as arm's length companies, and agencies operated at least in part by the public sector. Such arrangements can offer a more accessible source of comparison than outsourced services, as commercial providers are often somewhat coy about sharing their commercial arrangements. In all instances, your public sector peers could be a great source of accurate information, even if it sometimes has to be sanitised for commercial reasons.

The issue of value depends largely on who you ask. Ask existing public sector staff who are currently providing a service if they are offering a valuable and valued service, and they will almost invariably say yes. Ask members of the public disgruntled by a recent tax rise or perhaps a cut in public service, and you will elicit an entirely different answer. And while a particular service may be valued locally in the eyes of both local politicians and residents, that same service may not receive as much support from national government or perhaps from residents of an area in a different part of the country. Or ask local residents who have recently experienced the consequences of not paying their council tax on time or someone who has recently received a payment demand from HMRC – from their viewpoint, the term 'value' may have a different meaning.

So you will need to understand the different value systems of each group, and develop a model robust enough to navigate between the extremes. But beware of producing a value model that simply averages out extremes – this will not serve your purpose.

Ultimately, it will be for you, the service manager, in the light of your experience, local knowledge, local awareness of constraints and alternatives, to make a judgment as to how you think people value your service. And then you will need to ask them to validate your assumptions. Be warned – you could be dismayed when you ask them at the next stage, 'Reportage'. You could simply make assumptions based on your years of providing the service, but that would not be wise, and you could receive a rude shock when you ask the public or your clients about the value of your service.

The point here is to be able to identify which parts of your process or service delivery are those that are valued, welcomed – CHERISHed. You need to identify why people value them and then seek to ensure your delivery arrangements are built up around that value, so that when you move on to the next stage and take your pitch to the public or your client, you will have honed your 'what?', 'how much?' and value propositions.

What is really difficult to assess is the strength of public attachment to services visibly delivered by the public sector. If people see their local services delivered by a multitude of contractors, some of them global players, does this tend to weaken their loyalty to, and identification with, them? And to CHERISH them any less? Well, by way of example, most people would still firmly identify and value their GP as being part of the NHS, even though the majority of GPs have been operating as individual businesses and partnerships for many decades.

Evaluation specifics

You need to identify a range of comparators with similar and/or alternative service provision. That information must be gathered in a way that allows meaningful comparison of different ways of delivering the service, so that you can include this in your pitch to the public or internal clients. In gathering that information, you must consider the possibility that those you are pitching to may have had access to the same, or indeed better, information than you have. Consider the impact of you delivering your pitch having ignored or not been aware of some relevant comparison, and your audience having information that blows a hole in your carefully crafted pitch – not a position you would want to be in. So you will have to work hard to identify the widest possible indicators and comparisons you can so that that does not happen.

Your most basic tool for evaluation will be a critical analysis that considers questions such as:

- How have we done compared with last year?
- How have we done compared with our neighbours/our peers/our comparison reference group?
- How do we compare with the upper quartile/lower quartile/average service?
- Could we do this in a different way?
- Do our costs and outputs represent best value when measured against other available alternatives?

Your own set of questions and your framework will need to take into account your own local circumstances. The Method Study framework discussed earlier will be of particular use to you. Extending that to the next level of questioning will help you identify the questions you need to ask and then answer.

Admittedly, it can sometimes be very difficult to benchmark against alternative provision arrangements, particularly in the private sector. Commercial providers will often be guarded about providing costs and details of delivery arrangements without some guarantee of a delivery contract at the end of your discussions. And as we know, in the public sector, procurement of service provision must be open and transparent. This often takes a long time, so you will need to develop medium and long-term plans to move towards improved delivery arrangements if your investigations and evaluation indicate that it is the only way to offer true value. This may put you at odds with your organisation if they are not disposed towards such an option, but the New Public Sector will demand change and however you deliver your outcome, it needs to represent the best value you can achieve. Remember my example earlier of 'hybrid benchmarking'? In that example, the public sector managed to deliver savings that resulted in costs broadly equating to the private sector, but in a way that avoided procurement costs and much disruption.

Your CHERISH Champions may be able to make suggestions about appropriate benchmarking and comparisons with your own services, and it might be worthwhile investing in some professional advice from organisations who specialise in making comparisons. Whichever route you decide on, you will need to make sure the data you gather is sufficiently robust and suitable for your purpose. The last thing you want is to make comparisons that do not stack up under scrutiny.

We have often heard the term 'tough choices' being used as something of a mantra in both the previous and the current government. Most people understand the notion that resources are scarce but the demand for services limitless. In this context, there is potential for your evaluation process to send out infinite ripples as you try to get to grips with the relative values of competing claims on your budget.

You must beware of being driven to distraction by thinking about THE solution to these ramifications. There are limits to how long you can and should spend gathering meaningful comparisons. There is no precise or exact answer to the question. Even the apparently 'perfect' solution of letting the market decide on what represents the best cost and value is not the panacea many would have you believe. The market will change over time – often over a relatively short time – and the five-year contract you signed up to may end up looking expensive or outdated very quickly. That is not to say such arrangements do not have their place in delivering public services.

So the best suggestion I have for avoiding overanalysis is that you should clearly map and rank your options, overlay those options with the respective risks and benefits that would arise from changes to your service, and then test the concept with your CHERISH Champions. Bearing their advice in mind, draw a firm boundary round a finite area of interest. Beyond a certain point, it will not be practicable to assess too many alternatives, and certainly not within your 12-week deadline.

Sounding out the public

Visible and demonstrable engagement with the public is the essential next step and we will consider how you do this in the next section, 'Reportage'. At the same time, you will need to keep your eye on the austerity landscape, as it is changing almost by the week. The aim of the austerity agenda is clear even if the precise timing and route by which it is to be achieved may change. So it will be important for you to understand the local austerity context for your service, and to monitor what it is likely to mean this year, next year and in future years.

Unfortunately, even the biggest harvest of low-hanging fruit is not likely to deliver reductions that meet your challenging budget reductions. There will be some difficult choices, and the comparisons you will need to make will change as the New Public Sector emerges. Public expectation may change and that change will probably not be static. So you and other public sector managers will need to be brave, and will need to take the plunge and get the public's feedback more often.

The one thing that is true is that all public services across the land will be in the glare of someone's searchlight, whether that is the public's, your chief executive's or the Chancellor's. While you are doing all this digging around to determine what people value and what alternatives exist, take the opportunity to pick up on the 'mood music' around a particular service through social media and direct engagement. In fact, if you are not already monitoring what is being said about you online, you probably should not be in the public service! And if nothing is being said, well, you need to generate those conversations.

Remember, too, that not everyone is online, so do not restrict your search to that medium. Do not neglect local newspapers, local phone-in shows on radio, public meetings, even shopping centres and doctors' surgeries, and a myriad of other ways of engaging with those who use your service to discover the spontaneous assessments they make of your service.

How will I know if I have got there?

You really need to be sure that you have comprehensive comparison material before moving on to the next step. This section has highlighted some of the options you have for identifying suitable evaluation comparisons with your own costs and your proposed service delivery model, but you may well be able to come up with others.

The number of alternatives to your services is potentially infinite, so, as with previous stages, you will need to decide when you have enough information to give you confidence that you can stand in front of your public or your clients and not look foolish. In context, this means having sufficient understanding of your own costs and delivery arrangements (resulting from completing the 'Clarity' and 'How Much?' stages of CHERISH), having identified sufficient alternatives to allow people to make their own comparison.

Too little comparison will lead people to the conclusion that you have something to hide and have not brought them all the available information. Too much comparison will lead people to think you are trying to bamboozle them with data – because you have something to hide. So you will need to test the level of information you are providing before you place yourself in front of the public or your internal clients.

You will most certainly have taken a 360^0 perspective on your evaluation and comparisons. You will have examined the value of your service from the full range of stakeholders. I would suggest a minimum of three comparisons of similar activity, both in terms of cost and in terms of the value placed on them by customers and other stakeholders, and usually no more than six.

As I have mentioned before, CHERISH is an iterative process, and again, you will need to draw on your CHERISH Champions for robust challenge. Just as in the process of scientific enquiry you have to be looking for evidence that disproves your theory as zealously as you look for the evidence that proves it, you must expose the outcome of your evaluation to the most sceptical line of enquiry you can find. Bear in mind that you might even want to re-examine the composition of your CHERISH Champions to be sure that collectively they have the scope to scrutinise all aspects of your evaluation.

After all, this is the last stage before you go into the 'Arena of Austerity', so you will want to be well equipped to defend yourself! Be prepared too for knockbacks: you may have to go away, refine certain aspects of the evaluation, and try again.

Time to invoke Nietzsche's famous quote: "That which does not kill us, makes us stronger!"

Section 4: REPORTAGE

What does 'reportage' mean?

This section is about bringing together all you have done during the 'Clarity', 'How Much?' and 'Evaluate' stages and presenting your service to the public or to your clients. This is the stage of CHERISH where you get to test how far people value your service, so it is just about the most important stage in the whole CHERISH process. This is why an early word of encouragement is appropriate.

There are quite a number of synonyms for the term 'reportage' in *Roget's Thesaurus*. The ones I like most, and that most accurately get across what I mean when I refer to reportage, are communication, narrative, coverage, description, broadcast and information. I would go further and add words like consultation, dialogue, engagement, and feedback, although none of those words provides the whole story. In this section, I describe what I mean by reportage and what you need to do to ensure you take a compelling pitch to your audience. You can always add your own words to the list above, to make the description you generate personal and local to your service.

You need to use a range of methods to make sure you reach the people whose views you want, to engage with them in a way that is meaningful to them, and to gather their views about what you have told them. I have mentioned before that this is not 'consultation' in the classic public sector sense; that tends to have a quite specific meaning. Reportage is all about undertaking and demonstrating meaningful engagement that involves two-way dialogue and results in someone making a decision about your service – a CHERISH or PERISH decision. This is somewhat different from the existing public sector way of doing things, but likely to be a key part of the New Public Sector.

Reportage also involves using the widest range of media available, including 'traditional' means of communication such as face-to-face meetings and public events, leaflets, partner or third-sector liaison etc. But it also means becoming more comfortable and familiar with online means of engaging with people, using forms of communication and engagement that did not exist even five years ago. For many in the public sector these methods may be daunting, but it is a sobering thought that to get anything across to someone under 25, you are likely to have to engage their attention in the first five seconds or you will have lost them.

Deploying a combination of traditional and online methods will maximise your opportunity to engage with as wide an audience as possible. Online engagement will probably entail you becoming more familiar than you currently are with social media. While we all tend to think of the more common forms of social media, such as Facebook and Twitter, there are many other options. Think about blogs, alternative social media platforms in common use (such as Instagram), online surveys (such as SurveyMonkey) and other 'accelerating transaction' models that progressively and increasingly engage your audience. On the website www.newpublicsector.com you will find a ready-made 'Arena of Austerity' specifically designed for the public sector to showcase its services. It will also enable all the public services undertaking the CHERISH journey to 'pitch' against one another. Dedicated sites such as this allow public sector managers to expose their services to the widest possible public scrutiny at zero cost, and the more public services join the Arena, the greater the audience ready to comment on those services.

You will also want to consider the benefits of non-written media and the power of short videos about your service, or perhaps just you explaining clearly what your service does – delivering your pitch, in fact. In the Clarity section, I outlined the need to make sure you knew your pitch, were comfortable with it, and could deliver it in any situation. Well, why not make the most of the work you have put in by providing an online recording of that pitch using video and podcast? Consider the uptake and usage patterns of YouTube, and you begin to realise just how much the world has gravitated towards online media.

But as we know, not all of your audience use only online media. Many will prefer slower and more traditional forms of engagement, and many may prefer the option to mix formats.

Reportage is therefore all about finding the right medium through which to identify and approach your audience. It is about undertaking your engagement and making your pitch using your selected medium. And it is about gathering the evidence you already have and using the feedback to improve further.

While this stage is very important and potentially quite stressful, do not be tempted to defer it until later. It is important you do not become so worried about engaging with the public or your clients that you never get to complete this stage. And do not be put off by methods of engagement you may not understand, particularly the online options. There are many people available whose skills and experience you can draw on to undertake meaningful engagement using modern methods.

By the time you have got to this stage, you will have developed much greater clarity on what your service offers people and how much it costs, and you will have greater insight on how your service compares with alternative delivery arrangements. As a result, you will be better placed to explain to people why they should value your service. In fact, you are already very well placed to deliver this stage and achieve a positive result.

But even after all your explanation, the people you pitch to have a right not to endorse your service, and they may not feel sufficiently motivated to CHERISH it, so you will need to bring everything you have learned together in the most appropriate way and make sure you give it all you have to win the approval of your audience. While I dearly hope your audience will embrace what you pitch to them, if they do not, you will gain valuable feedback and insight about their thinking and opinions, and you will have an opportunity to re-present your service in the light of their feedback. This is a step you need not fear or delay unnecessarily. I have used the word 'brave' a number of times already, and this stage definitely requires you to display bravery.

The other key outcome of the Reportage stage will be gathering the evidence to provide to those leading the austerity drive in your part of the public sector. That evidence may be sufficient to persuade them that your service delivers its outcomes so efficiently and engages with its clients so effectively that they will approve what you have done and move on to easier targets. But you should not count on that.

Any austerity drive involves decisions that may not appear logical or rational, and this one is no different. No one can rule out your service being identified as one that is no longer required. Unfortunately, that is the nature of austerity and the shape of the New Public Sector. However, not having that evidence will almost certainly place your service at even greater risk and leave it more exposed to uncontrolled changes. Completing the Reportage stage is necessary to gather the evidence that your service is efficient, fit for purpose and CHERISHed.

What do I need to do?

Audience and media segmentation

The first thing you need to do is to understand the options you have in the way of engagement methodologies and to understand, or segment, your target audience. Then you need to bring the two activities together so that you apply the right techniques in the right way to the right people. That may seem very simplistic, but unless you understand both your audience and your techniques, you could end up wasting a lot of valuable time and resource.

The good news is that there are likely to be people in your organisation who understand how to do this. They should be able to offer you advice and support. Find them, explain what you are doing and what you want to achieve and then engage them in helping you with your journey. Look for alternative ways to deliver what you want. While many public sector organisations lead the way on engagement techniques, some may deploy more traditional techniques or may be after different outcomes from you. By all means canvass support from your organisation's communications and engagement teams, but make sure you also explore for yourself alternative and innovative ways to put your service in front of your audience and obtain direct feedback.

This could involve you engaging your CHERISH Champions as well as exploring new techniques for yourself. Find out what peer organisations have done, engage with sector, industry and professional networks and colleagues to see if they have developed methods you could adapt and deploy.

You first need to consider the nature and context of your service, of your audience and of your organisation. For example, if you are running a local service, you will obviously need to make sure that your engagement with your audience is identifiably rooted in their locality, but you also need to open your eyes to the ideas and opinions that come from outside your area. No one group has a monopoly of good ideas. For most local people, the detailed requirements of demands from Whitehall and their impact on other areas of the country may be of little interest. However, no one can afford to ignore the impact that austerity will have on them personally or their community. Few in the country will not have heard the term 'austerity' and considered all that that might mean for their public services.

You will want to appear calm and in control in the face of that austerity to persuade your audience that you have plans in place to ensure continuing delivery of their services to a high standard. But it may be useful to invoke the national picture in order to engage (and possibly enrage) people, so that they are willing to participate in a high-profile local initiative to generate conversation. You will want to avoid any impression you are responding to diktats handed down from Whitehall, but hinting that you are resisting them could harness the passion and anger so keenly felt in some parts of the country. While you should always approach such a situation carefully, you are offering your audience a ready-made outlet for genuine passion about your service.

For public sector managers with regional or national services, you will need to develop a different set of engagement techniques. Local services often do not have the same governance arrangements as national services, but you can mirror the techniques and approach outlined above. You may need to tailor your approach to engagement by soliciting views on a national service, but framed to incorporate local user voices or local delivery. Most national delivery bodies will have their own approaches to engagement, but this does not mean you should not seek better and more nimble ways to develop dialogue. You will have to judge for yourself how you can develop new ways of doing things in your particular organisation.

What every manager should have is a comprehensive overview of the composition of their audience, and of the means of communication appropriate for each part of that audience. You will need to think about how you 'segment' your audience and identify where they are, what they listen to and read, who they associate with, how they want to be engaged and how they might want to give you feedback.

You may want to consider investing some time looking at available social segmentation systems. There are many around, and the classic market segmentation systems used for years, based along the ABC lines, no longer apply. We are, apparently, much more sophisticated now and such simplistic systems do not accurately describe our habits and consumption. Luckily, there are 'consumer classification' systems available to help, for example, systems such as Acorn. I have provided a brief description of what such systems do, but you can find out more at www.acorn.caci.co.uk. Other similar systems are also available.

Developed by CACI Limited, the Acorn system is a segmentation tool that categorises the UK's population into demographic types. It examines demographic data, social factors, population and consumer behaviour to provide a far more nuanced understanding of different types of people, the pressures they face and their priorities. Based on the data, Acorn divides households, postcodes and neighbourhoods into six categories, 18 groups and 62 types. With information about this segmentation, you can target your service delivery far more accurately and find out what kind of improvements it is likely to need. The descriptions used by Acorn are shown below, and for each of the 18 groups a number of types is given.

Acorn Category	Acorn Groups	'Types'*
Affluent Achievers	Lavish Lifestyles Executive Wealth Mature Money	13
Rising Prosperity	City Sophisticates Career Climbers	7
Comfortable Communities	Countryside Communities Successful Suburbs Steady neighbourhoods Comfortable Seniors Starting Out	13
Financially Stretched	Student Life Modest Means Striving Families Poor Pensioners	15
Urban Adversity	Young Hardship Struggling Estates Difficult Circumstances	11
Not Private Households		3

*Number of 'Types' (sub-categorising the 'groups')

FIGURE 12: Acorn population segmentation

Acorn and similar systems have the advantage of being able to supply you with this information whether you are working at a national, local or regional level, so you do not need direct, first-hand knowledge of the geographical areas under consideration. It could be that your organisation already uses such a system to provide detailed information on its audience, so it is worth investigating this with your communications and engagement colleagues. Irrespective of whether you use a formal system or not in your CHERISH journey, understanding and applying the principles of systems like Acorn will help you in your thinking about how to segment your audience, and to ensure you match the messages to the group.

The matrix below is only a starting point for your analysis, and I have included a template at www.newpublicsector.com that you can populate for yourself. Bear in mind that this is only intended to be a general guide and you will need to tailor the segmentation descriptions to suit your own service and your own local circumstances. You can better understand the way each 'type' interacts and behaves by reference to the Acorn data at the link above. So having reviewed that information, consider whether it would be appropriate, for example, to send leaflets to the 'affluent achiever' category, given their preferred methods of engagement, or whether it would be appropriate to use online means to engage effectively with those in the 'urban adversity' category.

Media	Affluent Achievers	Rising Prosperity	Comfortable Communities	Financially Stretched	Urban Adversity	Not Private Households
Press – quality	●	●	●			
Press – tabloid			●	●	●	●
Magazines	●	●	●	●		
Radio – national	●	●	●			
Radio – local		●	●	●	●	●
TV			●	●	●	●
Online	●	●	●	●	●	
Email	●	●	●	●		
Mobile	●	●	●	●	●	●
Social Media	●	●	●	●	●	●
Outdoor	●	●	●	●	●	●
Cinema	●	●	●			
Direct Mail	●	●	●	●	●	
Street leafleting			●	●	●	●

FIGURE 13: Matching messages matrix

This segmentation may change the way you think about your audience, and you will clearly need to apply different thinking if your clients are essentially internal. Do not forget about members of your external audience that do not neatly fit into consumer or lifestyle categories, such as businesses, societies, and other organisational bodies and groups. Whatever means you decide are appropriate, there comes a point where you actually need to start your engagement process.

Remember, too, that there is an important message to get across about the difference between statutory services and discretionary services. In the 'good years' it will have been all too easy for people to assume that public bodies are obliged to deliver some services that simply fall into the category of 'nice to have'. Library services are a classic example of this: at one time it was a near-universal expectation that local authorities would provide universal access to books, and libraries were benchmarked on many things, including access times and book types. Now, however, the majority of people have access to books 100% of the time online, should they want it, not just through the local library. Your messages will need to allow for different responses about services that are mandatory – remember too that not everyone welcomes such services.

Setting up an NHS Patient Board

An NHS England client in London wanted to set up a Patient Board they could use to engage with as part of a challenging service transformation programme. When we advertised for members of the public to come forward and give their time to represent patients and the public, we were unprepared for the variety of respondents we got: everyone from ex-chief executives of Primary Care Trusts through to people with a mortal fear of dentists. We did not segment them in any way, we just capitalised on the strength of their engagement. You can be sure the Board collectively provided some fearlessly different perspectives, and this is exactly what was required. The mix of people made sure that this was a truly public voice, not mere output from either a room full of accountants, or a room full of anarchists. Try to follow that line so at least you will be making decisions in possession of the widest range of views possible.

Undertaking the reportage

Once you have completed your segmentation and decided on the most appropriate means of contacting each group, I have assumed you will go on to develop material and content to suit each option you have identified. Preparing appropriate material deserves a book in its own right, so I have made the broad assumption that you will complete that task to the highest standard possible within your time and budget constraints. A word of warning on this matter: make sure the material you provide for people is the best you can get. Your approach to people will influence their opinion of your organisation as a whole. Adhering to corporate communication and engagement standards is essential, and maintaining your organisational 'brand' is very important.

Your biggest challenge will be to come up with a request for responses that does not end up being the equivalent of inviting 'turkeys to vote for Christmas'. This is where your research into opportunity costs and options will empower your audiences to give informed thought to matching levels of service to levels of need. Considered as a dialogue, Reportage is not all one way. Some of the most powerful narratives will be those offered by those you are engaging with.

When it comes to the message itself, there are two areas to think about:

- The austerity narrative, and
- Your brand.

By and large, people have voted for austerity, and even if they have not, they appreciate that there is a majority who have. They have understood the analogy made with household budgeting (even though some would argue that it is not an entirely accurate one), so that narrative already exists in people's minds and should be invoked whenever possible.

The time you should allow for this stage will depend on your service and local circumstances. If you are using several channels of communication, you will need to consider how best you can manage them concurrently. The overall time for completing the CHERISH programme does not allow several weeks for each channel. You need to think smart and develop a timetable limited to four to five weeks' actual engagement. You may want to consider establishing a reference group within your CHERISH Champions to help you with that; you can use it to monitor progress and outcomes as they emerge. If you have time, you may want to create an audience-based reference group and have continuing contact after the Reportage stage ends, perhaps on a monthly or quarterly basis.

The benefit of a reference group is that you are able to get more than a snapshot of people's responses. But be aware that it can be very difficult to keep a fixed cast of people together to provide feedback on a continuing project. It may only be worth it for projects of extreme sensitivity, where there is a definite need to keep checking back at successive stages to be sure you are striking the right balance. You could come up with some sort of reward system to secure loyalty to the reference group.

Managing the Reportage activity will be challenging, and some aspects of it could be expensive if you seek external assistance. You will need to be absolutely clear about what output you want from each element of your engagement strategy. Keep in mind that the main requirement from this engagement is that your feedback should be genuinely representative and capture the views of as many of your audience as possible. The likelihood is that you will not capture the views of all your stakeholders, and the results and feedback you receive may not necessarily be what you expect (or want).

But I use the 'brave' word again here and managers who are afraid to ask the questions you are asking are not likely to survive.

The benefit of digital and online engagement methodologies is that they provide the opportunity for instant feedback and are relatively cheap to exploit. I have sought to harness that potential in the 'Arena of Austerity' mentioned earlier (www.newpublicsector.com), which is a virtual arena that draws on the power and reach of 'crowdsourcing' to identify and assess pitched services. The aim of the 'Arena of Austerity' is to mine public ideas and expertise through the participation of a million people. And a key part of that will be inviting public services to be judged by those people. The screenshots below demonstrate how this works.

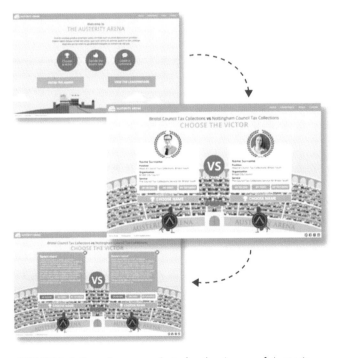

FIGURE 14: Sample screen shots for the Arena of Austerity

Public service managers are provided with space, free of charge, where they can publish their pitch, some accompanying video material and supporting information about their service. The system then selects two services at random and presents them in a competition to registered members of the public. They then select a 'winner' and decide if the winner should be CHERISHed. The site asks the audience for comments about each service, providing a simple means of gathering feedback and suggestions for future improvement. A 'leader board' identifies the services that are the most highly regarded. This is intended to be a quick, simple and effective way to showcase public sector services to as wide an audience as possible. While the intention is not to limit comment to an audience local to these services, the information provided in response to the pitch can be analysed, so that service managers can compare local and non-local responses and understand the differences.

So I would encourage you to visit the 'Arena of Austerity' and see what it can offer you and your service. The whole point of CHERISH is to identify people who will judge your service in terms CHERISH or PERISH, and this site takes that approach literally. Of course, this is not the only online tool in town, and you will need to find your own ways to reach out to those who are not 'wired' as well as to digital natives.

During the Reportage, you will need to monitor the progress in each of your engagement channels, and this is where online means can give you more immediate results. Whichever method you decide on, make sure you have also designed monitoring arrangements for the progress of this stage, so that you do not get to the end of your Reportage period only to be surprised by the quality of the response (or the lack if it). You may have identified absolutely the right platform through which to reach your audience, but it will count for nothing if what you have to say does not chime with them, and as a result they are not motivated to respond or to become involved.

Do not assume that just because you have put something out there, either by traditional means or online, people will know about it. We know that certain groups of people are difficult to reach for a variety of reasons. For some it is time, competing messages and perhaps lack of interest. For others it could be lack of access to computers, or understanding about the message, or reticence in responding. Many people wait for information be pushed at them rather than actively seeking it themselves, and today we have more information pushed towards us than ever before. So you will need to adopt a proactive approach during the engagement process and not be afraid of changing your plans if one route is not yielding results.

The final point you need to bear in mind is to remember that other people are not as immersed in your area of service as you are. They will be quick to spot any apparent contradictions between, for example, national and local messages, and perhaps between services in the same organisation or sector. The press will be quick to pick up on them too. Differences in approach between national and local government, or even between departments, can easily be mined for political gain, so do consider whether this would be a welcome consequence, or whether it could threaten to derail your brand.

Learning from feedback

Once you have completed your Reportage, you will need to assess the feedback you have received. Because each Reportage plan will be different, it is difficult to provide specific advice on what action you should take other than first to suggest you need to apply common sense and a sense of perspective. You have an opportunity to improve your service based on the feedback you have received, whether it fell in the upper or lower quartile of your expectations. The main thing is that you have completed the process and now have a much better understanding of what your stakeholders, audience and clients think about your service. Questions you may want to ask yourself when you have assessed the feedback you received may include:

- What was the overall outcome from your Reportage?
- Did your audience understand your message, your pitch, your service?
- Did your audience CHERISH your service? Did you ask them to CHERISH your service?
- Did your audience ask relevant questions or did the material you provided them with mean they were not as informed as you would have liked?
- Was your audience representative of all stakeholders or users? Were certain sections of your audience under-represented?
- What suggestions and feedback did your audience provide that could lead to further improvements?
- Did your audience raise issues or questions about your wider organisation and what were the implications of those issues?
- What aspects of your service did your audience like/dislike and do any features of your service stand out as requiring further investigation?
- What did your audience think about the comparisons you had provided and the level of detail on costs?

These are all relevant questions and there are likely to be many more you would want to add to that list to inform the next stage of

CHERISH, as you seek to identify further improvements. It may be that certain locations, or certain sections of your audience raised different, and perhaps, competing issues. The nature of public services is that competing interest groups will receive the same service. Go back to the Acorn information and look at the way they segment society. You may not agree with the descriptions of each grouping, but at least you will understand the differences they engender.

We will explore in the next section, 'Improve', what you will need to do with the feedback. But for now, I suggest you gather together all the feedback and information you obtained, review it, analyse it, understand it. Convene your CHERISH Champions and give them some initial feedback. Then pat yourself and your team on the back and get ready to do something about the feedback you received.

How will I know if I have got there?

You have got there if you have completed your Reportage and have obtained feedback from your audience, as set out in your engagement plan. That feedback may not be as complete as you wanted it to be or perhaps it does not contain the message you want, but you have completed the task you set for yourself. At the next stage, you will need to do something about that feedback, so do not get too complacent.

If you did all the groundwork suggested in this and earlier sections, you will have completed a comprehensive engagement process plan, with your sponsor(s) and CHERISH Champions all clear about the nature of their involvement and the timings for it. Your feedback and Reportage plan will have reflected a reasonable segmentation of your audience, given your time and resources, and you will have developed and provided fully worked-up messages crafted to suit the needs of those you were engaging with.

At the same time, you will have presented a persuasive, evidence-based case to those heading the austerity drive in your organisation, demonstrating efficient delivery of your service and effective engagement with clients.

You have got there if you feel confident that you have completed the above actions to the highest standard possible under your specific circumstances. The next step is to act on your feedback and perhaps offer yourself the luxury of thinking about the impossible. Austerity need not mean the end of inspiration! The question you must now ask yourself is, what more *could you have done* in the stages leading up to the Reportage? Suppose you were given a budget of £100k to undertake the work you have just completed and maybe an additional three months to do it in. What would you have done and how would you spend that budget? Would you have refined your pitch more? Would you have done more to identify greater efficiencies or savings? Would you have approached the Reportage stage differently?

Well, good news. Even if you do not have that £100k, you now have an opportunity to do things differently and you now have firm evidence from your audience to help guide further improvements. You may have tough messages to convey, and difficult stories to tell, and you will have to be braced for the responses. But you are in a solid place to drive through further improvements.

Section 5: IMPROVE

What does 'improve' mean?

The meaning of 'improve' is self-evident, but in your context there are questions you need to answer, such as:

- What shall I improve?
- Why should I improve it?
- How much do I need to improve?
- Who says I should improve?

In this section, we will explore what you can do to make things even better. You start this part of the CHERISH journey fresh from having engaged with your stakeholders on the service you propose to deliver to them. You took your offer to them. They responded and gave you feedback. You must, therefore, take this as your starting point to answer these 'what?', 'why?', 'how much?'' and 'who says?' questions.

Your stakeholders, no doubt, will have given you plenty of food for thought. If they decided your service and delivery arrangements were very good, they may have even designated you as a CHERISHed service. If so, very well done. If your feedback was less enthusiastic, you have improvements to make based on your audience's feedback.

But even if you received top marks, this still does not mean you can afford to be complacent. Remember the fluid nature of the New Public Sector and the need for continuous improvement.

I will start by making a broad assumption that the feedback you received indicated you had some improvements to make. Obviously, I cannot predict the outcome for your particular service; I can only try to provide general guidance on what you need to do in order to make it even better. The New Public Sector will assume no service remains static. You cannot sit back unless you have next year's improvement plan in the bag, ready to go at a moment's notice.

An excellent book by Lucy Gower, *The Innovation Workout: The 10 tried-and-tested steps that will build your creativity and innovation skills*, provides some great examples of the challenges of improvement for all service managers. Lucy emphasises the difficulty all managers have, irrespective of sector, in predicting 'the next big thing'. She advises that while we may all have a hunch about the next few weeks, months or even a year, it is impossible to predict much beyond that, because so many forces are at play, in a continuous flux. Local and global economics, politics (with both a small and a large 'p'), developments in technology, new product inventions that change consumer behaviour, weather patterns, celebrity fads, a one-off breakthrough. Maybe even the next equivalent of the World Wide Web could serve as a 'giant curveball thrown into the constantly changing mix'.

As we all know, the world has never changed so fast. The New Public Sector is not exempted from such change, and for many public sector managers, their service could well be at the leading edge of that change. In the context of identifying further improvements you could make in your service, the best you can do is to focus first on what you want to achieve and be alert to your changing environment. Lucy's view is that there are no blueprints for predicting the

110

next big thing, but she suggests the following tips for how to be ready to sniff out the next opportunity when it presents itself:

- **Remember that no idea operates in a vacuum:** Get into the habit of spotting what is happening by keeping up with social, economic and environmental trends. Developments in these areas work together to shape change, so what is happening today will inform future trends.
- **Look for the trends that have not affected your business yet:** For example, what would the impact be if you knew that mobile phones were going to be the only method of payment in the future? What would that mean for how you develop your products and services?
- **Study the data:** What can you learn from your data? What patterns, trends and associations can you make from analysing the data you already have?
- **Make it a habit:** If you want to get good at anticipating and responding to trends, as with any professional development, you have to practise. Find a way to make the above activities a habit. Make regular time to think about the next big thing.

There is a specific chapter in Lucy's book that you might find very useful for its practical advice on understanding your environment and predicting the trends of tomorrow. Horizon scanning may be nothing new for most public sector managers, but some of the ideas in this chapter are really innovative.

In deciding on the scope of the improvements you intend to deliver, you will need to consider your own particular context and that of your service, your organisation and your environment. Austerity may be something of a buzzword right now and is likely to remain so for several years, but at some point, it will be replaced by something new, but which will nevertheless probably incorporate basic assumptions of austerity and performance improvement as givens – and some form of public sector service 'deflator'.

This section therefore provides some guidance on how best to go about preparing for that, and how that preparation fits into the Improve part of your current CHERISH journey. By way of example, here is a short case study of performance improvement at the start of the era of 'scientific management'.

Maximum efficiency

Frederick W. Taylor was an American inventor and engineer, and is considered the father of 'scientific management'. His influential theory enabled industry to move away from management by 'rule of thumb' and be more efficient and prosperous. He had some very clear yet simple ideas that continue to form the basis for many improvement processes, including increasing specialisation and division of labour and systematically analysing the relationship between workers and tasks, enabling redesign of processes to ensure maximum efficiency. One of his more memorable suggestions was to give workers 'bigger shovels so more grain could be lifted with each action.'

What do I need to do?

Equipped with your feedback, you can now identify what you need to change to satisfy your public, your stakeholders and those driving the austerity agenda in your organisation.

You will have been working collaboratively all the way, with the endorsement of your sponsors, taking soundings through your Champions, consulting your stakeholders and finally engaging with the public. So you will now have a pretty good view of what would represent 'improvement' in the eyes of all these interested parties. And the feedback you will have received during Reportage will either reinforce your views on the service you are delivering or cause you to radically reassess what your audience wants. As I cautioned earlier, certain statutory services will inevitably be unpopular, so keep adverse comments on such services in perspective. Some outputs will never be palatable, however much you improve the means of delivery!

The difficulty is that, depending on the circumstances of your service, 'improvement' is likely to mean different things to different groups. Your challenge is to steer a course between these divergent expectations. Who said being a manager in the public sector was easy?

Take another look at the CHERISH diagram shown at Figure 1. Note that the diagram has a starting point but then becomes a continuous cycle. Now that you have an understanding of your baseline, you need to ensure you continue to progress from that point. And the next sections will identify how you can use your staff, stakeholders and audience to make that job easier.

Balancing perceptions of the further improvements you plan to deliver will be a delicate exercise. If you have already made improvements in the lead up to your Reportage, things may now start to get a little more difficult. While some parts of the press and those championing austerity might applaud the improvements you have in mind, it could be a different story at local level. For example, the perceptions of those who, say, always pay their council tax on time will differ from those who do not. The former will be delighted at any attempt to recover a greater proportion of council tax, while the latter may be indifferent, or even see any expenditure on such an exercise as throwing good money after bad. But in the end, you want to demonstrate that you are collecting as much as you can, as efficiently as you can.

Remember that one of the most perennial pieces of advice for people doing any kind of publicity or communications is that you should tell people what you are going to tell them, tell them it, and then remind them of what you have just told them. And then repeat the exercise all over again. It may appear like a war of attrition against negative perceptions and you may well be right.

Having just canvassed the opinion of your public or your clients, it would probably be sensible to spend a little time absorbing the feedback you received, refining your delivery plans, and working through your next steps before you go back to that same audience. Going back to people for their views too soon is likely to annoy them and may suggest that you did not listen to them in the first place. Avoid losing their goodwill by making sure that when you do go back to them, your pitch is noticeably different (and better) than it was before. In normal circumstances, I would suggest leaving at least five to six months before you go back to your audience, but that does not mean you cannot test improvements during that period.

114

Remember also that you are not operating in isolation. A squeeze in one area of your organisation may well mean a bulge in another. As a public service manager, you will always be operating in a wider system, so you must be astute enough to notice when you risk pushing through improvements to your service that might make you look good, but at the expense of your organisation or of other public services in your area. But if you find that your progress towards improvement is being blocked by the inaction of others, this needs to be flagged up within the organisation.

Improvement	What it might mean	Considerations
Doing more for less	• Identifying better delivery mechanisms (the 'larger shovel' solution) • Reducing duplication	• Solutions not necessarily easy to find • Workforce resistance to solutions
Doing the same for more people	• Extending a service so that the unit cost is less • Identifying a vehicle for wider delivery	• Risk of compromising quality of service • Cuts to services may mean reduced capacity elsewhere for sharing
Doing less for less	• Reducing the content of a service • Providing the service to fewer people through more accurate targeting	• Managing public expectation • Managing staff dissatisfaction • Managing impact on stakeholders and contractors
Doing the same more effectively	• Reducing the drop-out rate • Reducing repeat service demands	• Challenging client groups may make this option difficult

FIGURE 15: Sample feedback framework

So listen to the feedback from Reportage to give you an indication of what the public would like to see improved. Your mission, should you choose to accept it, will be to map this onto the intelligence you have been receiving from CHERISH Champions about what stakeholders think, and onto your perceptions and knowledge of what is required in terms of budgets. What the public proposes is likely to fall into certain broad categories of improvement, and the table above gives a few illustrative examples of what you may have received in the way of feedback. You will want to prepare your own framework so it reflects your specific feedback.

Where people have clearly registered dissatisfaction with a service, you will need to do some analysis into its shortcomings to identify your targets for action. You must consider the extent of resources available, taking into account the austerity agenda within your own organisation as well as more widely across the public sector.

The notion of 'fit for purpose' also comes into play here, particularly in the context of local services, where communities in different parts of the country have very different priorities. It is fair to say that the priorities of, for example, residents of Rotherham may not be the same as those of Mole Valley. Local variations in devolved areas of the country – Scotland, Wales and Northern Ireland and, soon to be, large areas of the North of England – will be different again, resulting in a different dynamic in demand for improvement compared with other areas. Tolerance of low-level crime, for example, is likely to be far higher in a densely populated urban setting than it would be in a leafy suburb or rural area. In this example, the police presence required to crack down on such crime might be considered heavy-handed and intrusive in a city neighbourhood, whereas it would be welcomed as reassurance in a suburban or rural setting. Your improvement plans therefore have to accommodate your audience as well as reflect what you are charged with delivering.

Inevitably, you will find yourself having to contend with opposing views within a locality. Regeneration, for example, can also generate conflict in a neighbourhood. Local bikers in Battersea, London, soon found themselves embattled when the residents of a newbuild block complained about their regular biker gatherings at a local café, attracting their compadres from miles around, despite the practice having being a feature of the area for many years.

I am sure I do not have to convince you of the merits of preparing clear improvement plans. It is essential to have a shared document that sets out who is meant to be doing what, when and in what order. You will have to prepare your own timetable for making the further improvements happen and then for going back to your audience again – and then back again to the 'Arena of Austerity' to ask for your service to be CHERISHed.

You will have to decide for yourself when to stop this cycle. You must always keep improving, but without risking too much audience engagement on the same topic. Going back to people several times is unlikely to win their trust or the approval of your superiors. Approach re-engagement sensibly.

The other benefit of improvement plans is that they help to keep everyone working towards goals agreed in black and white and help to avoid mission creep, which is a perennial danger, especially if you are working in a multi-disciplinary or multi-agency setting.

Your CHERISH Champions can provide valuable input at this stage by sounding out stakeholders as you develop your refined improvement plan and the timetable for re-engagement. Stakeholders and partners will probably not be 'backwards in coming forwards' with their feedback, but you cannot expect to have the same level of input from the public. People have a lot competing for their time these days, so the reality is that they may give you decreasing attention every time you approach them. You need to develop a balance between never engaging and engaging constantly (which your audience would find rather wearing), depending on the nature of your service. So, for example, if you deliver community policing services, you may well want to assess public reaction constantly by monitoring social media. But if you are a council tax collection service, seeking feedback every 18 months or so (unless you are introducing massive changes to the process) will be enough. Design your Improve and 're-Reportage' timescales around your audience's tolerance as well as your own needs.

Even when they are not actively gathering feedback, the CHERISH Champions can make sure you continue to keep your partners and stakeholders up to date with what is being planned, so no one can claim that they were not informed of changes and developments.

How will I know when I have got there?

In words not 100% faithfully reproduced from Confucius, the only way you are ever going to know whether you have got there is if you know where you started from, by which I mean you need to have a very clear baseline. The good news is you now have that firmly established. You know what your audience wants and expects. Keep an eye, as best you can, on the austerity agenda too. Become more aware of what is going on locally as well as nationally so you know what is heading your way.

Equipped with that understanding, you can plan your further improvements effectively and know exactly where you started from and where you need to be. You will know you are there when you have got sign-off from your sponsors and you start delivery. But most importantly, you will know you are there when your audience awards you CHERISHed status. Both are great yardsticks for confirming that you are on track. But as I have said before, do not expect those driving austerity to take notice only of those measures. You must go further, and in the next sections we will be looking to export your approach to others and enable them to apply it to their areas of business, so you need to know what you did, how you did it and how you can pass it on to others.

If you also have other services or colleagues beating a path to your door to ask you for advice as to how you achieved your improvements, that too is a sure sign you have done something right. This is all part of the 'Share' and 'Help' stages that form the next two sections.

For some services, some form of government recognition could be an ultimate accolade and the source of that merit will depend on where you are in the public sector and where you are in the country. Do publicise the progress you are making, perhaps through case studies, which will put your service on the map and contribute to local and national improvement programmes.

Assuming you have got there, do not keep it to yourself.

Of course the realistic answer, faintly daunting but also optimistic, has to be that *you will never get there*. Remember, we did not decide that we had completed the improvement of the wheel when we put a solid rubber tyre around it. Improvement will have to continue to meet the successive needs of a changing society, and it will help you to emerge as a leader in the New Public Sector.

Section 6: SHARE

What does 'share' mean?

Having done the 'external groundwork' required to get your message to the widest possible stakeholder audience, you now need to make sure those delivering your service 'live your brand'. That is a term much used in the private sector to describe how organisations deploy their staff, their partners and other stakeholders to spread a CHERISHed message at every opportunity.

This section will describe how you can do that within a public sector context. I recognise that public services are not soap powders, cars or chocolate bars, so they require a different approach to 'brand management'. But whether a public service is local or one offered nationally, each has its own distinct brand, ways of doing things, ways of interacting with its audience, and look and feel.

The good news is that most of the groups of people you need to harness to help you deliver this have already been involved in developing your pitch. They should already know about the message you want them to share. This section focuses specifically on how you can use those groups of people, and others, to work on your behalf. While that may sound simple, you will still have to put in some hard work to make sure you earn the trust of those who will act as brand and service 'advocates' on your behalf.

The corporate world is littered with case studies of organisations that took the loyalty of their staff and partners (and indeed their customers) for granted, to their great cost and often demise. You will have your own examples, I am sure, of organisations and brands you once valued but who lost their way, or failed to delight you once too often, or perhaps stopped meeting your needs. And equally, you will also have your own examples of organisations you moved to because your friend, family member or neighbour said they were really happy with the service they received, or maybe you read about the company in the press or on social media.

You need to capture the goodwill you have surrounding your service and harness it to best effect. I will try to identify ways you can do that without a large corporate budget, using only the resources you already have available.

What do I need to do?

Not delivering on your core service 'offer' is one of the worst things you can do in a service-related industry. (It is not great in manufacturing and consumer goods either, quite frankly.) In service provision, you may be able to gloss over a less-than-excellent service once or twice. Yes, you may be able to win over your audience with great promises only to let them down when it comes to delivery. In many instances, it will be the staff delivering the service that will be your weakest link. People like dealing with people, and at some point in your delivery arrangements, your staff will interact with your customer base, your audience. Some public services have moved to more online delivery over recent years, so have less human-to-human interaction. Such services work well when they work and are very cost effective, but we are still a long way from the point where all public services can be delivered by such methods. Generally, at least some element still relies on a human input.

One of the key things you need to do, therefore, is make sure your staff, your delivery partners and your stakeholders are enthusiastic, knowledgeable – passionate even – about your service. And you need to make sure that that passion is well placed and well founded. Having very enthusiastic staff and a pretty mediocre service is not the road to being CHERISHed, so you need to develop systems and processes that ensure that your service delivers in the real world.

First things first. In the previous sections we determined that you now have clarity on your service, know exactly how your numbers stack up, understand the true significance of your service both to your users and other stakeholders, and have sounded out the public about their views on your service. You now also have an improvement plan in place.

In getting yourself to this position, you are likely to have gathered around you a bunch of engaged and committed CHERISH Champions with a keen understanding of what you are trying to do. It is also highly likely that some of your own staff will have been involved in that process, so now you need them all engaged in promoting and publicising your service.

Everyone in your organisational network (staff, partners, suppliers, stakeholders) needs to be aware of what you are doing and to act as an ambassador for your CHERISH project and for your service. The last thing you want is to get to the end of the CHERISH process and find that there are people out there claiming not to have heard about any of this – or worse, they have heard of it but they have heard bad things via your network.

Hopefully, the CHERISH Champions among your staff will already have been busy putting out some constructive messages and stories about what is afoot. This might not be easy, particularly if jobs and local services are on the line, but all those working in the public sector should be taking every opportunity they can to project a positive image of the changes brought about by austerity and to seek to address public concern proactively. Remember, those outside the public sector are often less than sympathetic to the plight of those working within it.

Despite the gung-ho attitude and spirit of openness among you and your CHERISH Champions, not all of your staff may fully embrace the positivity you feel about what you are doing. And some days, you and your CHERISH Champions may not feel as positive about it all as you do on other days. That is a normal part of the human condition and your staff deserve to be clear about what the CHERISH process will deliver for them, otherwise they cannot be open and honest with your audience. So I suggest you develop a clear and honest pitch for your staff about their prospects and the future of your service. Even if they might not like the message, it is better to be honest and open than to have a fudged message, or worse, one that is deliberately misleading.

As I described in the Reportage section, the private sector has developed a myriad of mechanisms for getting its messages out. Audience segmentation using the Acorn system gives you a flavour of such mechanisms. In the same way, such systems are used to locate and hone target client groups, so they are very effective for collating the opinions of each audience group. Commercial organisations spend a lot of money making sure their message or brand is correctly 'positioned' in the market and is received in the best way. Clearly, most public sector managers do not have those resources at their disposal, so you will need to adopt more pragmatic and practical ways of assuring your brand and service's positioning.

I would suggest using the same broad approach as you adopted in Reportage, with the same audience segmentation. You need to map those groups on to the interaction your staff, partners and stakeholders have with them, and then to develop a plan to exploit each interaction so that you waste no opportunities to engage public, client or stakeholders when your service is in front of them. Clearly, you will need to make sure your actions are appropriate – you are not selling soap powder or consumer goods, you are providing a public service and you do not need to adopt every commercial trick in the book. Become familiar with traditional and modern marketing and public relations techniques so you are at least aware of how commercial operations work and of the options at your disposal.

Your key assets are generally going to be your organisation, your public sector ethic and above all, strongly motivated and positive staff. You will need to decide the relative value of each of those assets and develop an appropriate sharing campaign based on your strengths. I have assumed there will be little money allocated in the New Public Sector for telling the public how good their public services are, but the power and voice of your staff can be harnessed to good effect. With appropriate forethought and planning, you should have many opportunities for getting your message out by engaging your staff.

Tailoring your messages

The precise messages you need to relay will vary enormously. You will need to reflect the feedback you received, your planned improvements and the context of your service. Who, after all, is likely to declare, 'Wow, yes, you really are the best council tax collection service in the land and I now realise that!"? OK, there are exceptions to everything and congratulations if you have received that type of accolade. But for most public sector managers, acceptance, recognition and satisfaction will be the route to becoming CHERISHed. There is no escaping the fact that it is that last elusive step motivating people to take your service to their hearts that is the most difficult. It is likely to be the same elusive step that will motivate your staff, similarly, to CHERISH the service they work in. If you can crack that nut together, they will want to tell others about it – it is human nature.

It will help if you can match your CHERISH Champions to particular groups of staff, and you should have a degree of ready-made leadership in this area. Similarly, if you have a trusted representative from one of your key stakeholders or providers that your staff have extensive contact with, it would make sense to find ways to co-opt that person into sharing your message. This brings an added bonus, in that such messages are often better received when they come from outside your organisation.

At a general level, your various messages will need to:

- Contain information that is relevant – staff in one sector will not want to be burdened with information that applies only to a team or unit remote from their own sphere of work. Also, seek to avoid annoying others with an overemphasis on your success at the expense of a focus on your outcomes.
- Encourage only as much engagement and feedback as your organisation can reasonably respond to – you need to be realistic about how much feedback your improvement plan and timetable can accommodate.

- Engage the heart, as far as possible – many people have chosen to work in the public service because they want to make a difference or to focus on a particular community, so make sure your message chimes with their thinking and values.
- Be honest – you may be surprised how disarming a straightforward message can be and you will have learned much about that leading up to your Reportage.

How will I know if I have got there?

The acid test for whether you have shared your plans for improving the service effectively with your staff is if any one of them could do a persuasive short pitch of, say, 30 seconds to a minute, about the proposals, their benefits, and why you should care about them.

And if you can elicit a genuine broad message from your staff that says something like, 'Yes, I am confident our service is as good as it can be, and we have a clear improvement path' then you are mostly there.

And if you can be confident your staff are delivering that message at every opportunity and delivering it with sincerity, then you are probably there. Inevitably, you will have some members of staff who are comfortable delivering such messages and some who may be less keen. That is fine, and if you reach the 'tipping point' of 51% of your staff delivering that message, that is a sign of success; anything north of that level is a bonus.

Be realistic about what you can expect your staff to deliver. Yes, they may be passionate about what they do, but people are not always comfortable discussing or displaying their passions. Respect that and see if there are different ways some staff can help deliver the message.

Ideally, all your staff will have a degree of knowledge beyond the basic message, but remember that not everyone will want to present their service. Nevertheless, a level of knowledge appropriate to the extent of their involvement with the service will be recognised by most people engaging with them. Nobody needs to know everything.

Although it may sound paradoxical, I would say that another sign that you have got there is if you have a degree of constructive challenge from your staff. This shows they feel they have a sound understanding of the issues, and, crucially, they feel empowered to engage with them critically. Some of the best ideas may be those that are coming out of left field, and the fact that you have provided a space for them to be aired is to your credit.

You also need to see among staff recognition that this time it is different. This time austerity is a serious threat to their futures and their livelihoods. They will see that you have chosen to do something about it even though you may have no real control over the outcome; you have not turned tail and buried your head in the sand.

Staff in all sectors of the economy can be forgiven for becoming cynical in the face of successive waves of management initiatives that may be taken up enthusiastically, become a bit of a nine-day wonder, and then sink without trace. The public sector has had its share, but take a look at the rest of the economy and you will realise you are not alone. Many organisations suffer from initiative fatigue. But the changes we need to see now are nothing to do with fashions in management and all to do with extreme necessity.

Austerity cannot be discarded on a whim, even if many in the public sector would want to do so. As a reality check, you could pick three companies, organisations, or even departments within your own organisation, whose practices you admire and then compare your CHERISH programme with their change programmes, by way of a soft benchmarking exercise. The context may be very different, but you can still identify key similarities between your way of proceeding and theirs in terms of processes, and assess how effective they have been in achieving their goals, capturing some valuable learning along the way.

Finally, remember that CHERISH is an iterative process and does not end with you ruling a line under improvement. The New Public Sector will demand that you never sit on your laurels and always strive to improve. The changes being delivered as a result of austerity will change the relationship between you and your public forever.

So if you arrive at this stage and feel that you have not quite got the engagement you hoped for, then revisit the earlier stages. Where you feel you are missing a key bit of evidence, go back and ask people outright. The processes you have set up will accommodate this.

If you are happy with where you are and your outcomes, then you should first of all be proud. But you should also have the zeal and enthusiasm to help other parts of your organisation or even those outside your organisation to get to the same point as you have got to. The next and final part of the CHERISH process, Help, outlines how you can go about that and, in so doing, raise your own profile and become one of the opinion formers in the New Public Sector.

Section 7: HELP

What does 'help' mean?

In the last section, we looked at sharing your chosen CHERISH project with staff and stakeholders throughout your organisation, so that both groups became advocates and brand ambassadors for your service. In this section, I want to take that a little further, so you now share your experiences more widely across the public sector.

My thinking here is that in a time of increasing austerity, and with the emergence of the New Public Sector, all public sector managers need to learn how to get by with less than they have had in the past. One of the simplest ways to do that is for everybody to learn from the experiences of others in the sector. This is a cost-effective way to spread the improvement message further than would normally be possible given limited resources. This section encourages you not to try to reinvent the wheel, nor to keep all your experience to yourself. Hoarding your expertise and knowledge at the expense of colleagues within your organisation, your sector or the wider public service is counterproductive. If you have a belief in the public service – and I am assuming you do if you have read this far! – I am pretty sure you will have the urge to improve the lives of its clients, be that your clients or the clients of a peer service.

What I have in mind is that once you have been through the CHERISH process yourself, you should be willing to become a bit of an advocate for positive change, making sure, of course, that you do this in the right way. This could mean offering to help other organisations, maybe further-flung units in your own organisation, or other groups in your peer network. Perhaps you have already identified people who have yet to embark on the CHERISH journey or who perhaps need to be nudged in the direction of improvement. Maybe you know people who have not thought as deeply as you have about the impact the New Public Sector could have on them and their career. I would go further and suggest that those you partner with, such as third and fourth-sector organisations, and perhaps suppliers, need to be made aware of this systemic change. I would add to that sentence 'always within the rules you need to adhere to on procurement and supply'.

But do not regard such assistance as a charitable or philanthropic endeavour. There are likely to be a variety of mutual benefits for both you and those you help. You will become known as a 'go-to' person willing and able to offer support to other public sector services and, as a result, your profile and that of your service will increase. You are also likely to identify additional benefits and improvements when you work with others, particularly if you are helping organisations outside your sector. There are many benefits to be had from joining up parts of the public sector that currently work in isolation or, at best, in a rather fragmented way. As you help others to improve, they in turn will help their colleagues to improve. Imagine if you could genuinely say to yourself that you set in train a whole series of improvements in your geographical area or your service area. That is what public service is about – sharing collective knowledge for the benefit of the public.

When two or more organisations come together to improve and share knowledge, it provides a useful opportunity to gain a fresh perspective on your own organisation. If, for example, an NHS organisation finds it holds information on usage patterns that may be valuable to third-sector organisations or local authorities, sharing it may enable overall planning and service delivery to improve at little cost. That has got to be a good thing in times of austerity and it is what those driving austerity refer to as 'smart thinking'.

Sharing data

Transport for London (TfL) is committed to syndicating open data to third parties where that is technically, commercially and legally viable. TfL actively engages private sector developers to deliver and innovate using its open data. To date, some 5,000 developers have registered to use its data, which has led to the development of high-quality travel applications, tools and services. Developers have created hundreds of applications, reaching millions of active users.

But why does TfL want to share its open data? Well, it takes the view that as it is held by a public body, its data actually is publicly owned. It also considers that its goals are better served by opening up this data, which means that anyone needing travel information about London can get it wherever and whenever they wish, in any way they wish. And interestingly, TfL sees the economic benefit that open data brings helping to develop technology enterprises, grow small and medium businesses, and generate employment and wealth for London and beyond.

When you help others, the organisations you support benefit from your experience, and you gain more knowledge. Developing a strong collective response to austerity could result in genuinely innovative activity for all. But I must emphasise that 'help' does not mean doing everything for the organisation you support. We will explore the importance of setting reasonable and mutual expectations for your offer to help. Recipient organisations in turn have a responsibility to deliver on their side of the agreement, otherwise the process will not work.

What do I need to do?

My advice is to start close to home and proceed outwards. You should be in a good position to approach other areas in your own organisation, or perhaps peer organisations in your professional network, directly. There is no limit to the number of organisations to which you can offer support other than the obvious constraints of your time and the tolerance of your own organisation. There is no reason why you should not promote your offer of help locally, regionally or nationally.

Your CHERISH Champions could help with this, or you could 'advertise' through the media relevant to your area of work, or you could even use the CHERISH forums that form part of the Arena of Austerity. That forum activity encourages an exchange of help for those who have gone through the CHERISH process using the Arena of Austerity and for those who have just started their journey by registering their interest. The web address for the Arena of Austerity is www.newpublicsector.com.

You can start identifying other organisations you think may need help at any stage during your CHERISH journey. You do not have to wait to the end. In fact, two peer organisations going through the journey together can offer each other a great deal of mutual support. That small informal arrangement could turn into something bigger if you decided the experience is a positive one.

The fit between the supported and the supporting organisations is important. An organisation is more likely to value your experiences and to relate to your outcomes if it is of a similar scale and if it shares at least some element of your culture. That does not mean there is a prescriptive model or framework you need to fit into. Start some conversations, tell people about the CHERISH programme, and make clear to them that it is not rocket science. Be open about your worries about austerity and the New Public Sector, and let them know that you have found a way to try to deal with what lies ahead. But be honest about the possibility that everything you have done may still be swept away. Above all else, tell them that at least you tried.

But beware of 'evangelising' to the point where people avoid you and be careful to set up reasonable expectations. There is a fine line between the passionate advocate and the obsessive zealot everyone hides from when you turn up at a conference! I strongly recommend spreading good news, a simple process and a positive outcome, but the CHERISH process is not 'snake oil', merely the application of common sense and hard data. When you are setting out a realistic offer of help to another individual, service or department, you hope your journey will prove attractive to people who can benefit from it, and who are prepared to participate actively.

So how many other services can you help at any one time? Well, I would be realistic and suggest you cannot hope to help more than three organisations at a time. You would probably want to start with one now and have a couple of others due to start a few weeks or months down the line. You may have to operate some sort of selection process in deciding who to help, whether you are approaching them directly or deciding between organisations who have volunteered to receive help.

Your selection process should be based on your capacity, capabilities, experience and interests, and how these all fit with the other organisation. Consider also the extent of their motivation. Are they bought into the CHERISH journey and the reasons they are embarking on it? Do they give you confidence they are likely to deliver a positive outcome that will reflect well on you and vindicate the time you have invested in them? Do they have the capacity and capability to go through the journey you have just gone through? How will their organisation react?

You will need to develop your own process to decide who to help. Your time is valuable and this is something you will be doing in addition to your day job, so do factor in the impact that the time spent helping others may have on your service.

And try not to 'bludgeon' other organisations or groups into taking up your offer, regardless of how much you think they may be in need of your help. As with all the stages of this process, you can adopt an iterative approach with, perhaps, a further offer in the future. Your experience will be refined and amended in the light of your experience of helping another organisation so maybe that new experience may persuade participation.

What help should you provide?

Once you have identified an organisation to help, you have assured yourself they are worthy of your time and your organisation has sanctioned you providing help, what do you do first?

As part of your sifting process, you should have been asking questions of the supported organisation to understand what they need from you, how they would like you to provide that and what kind of time commitment they can give. I would recommend you use that information to draw up an agreement defining the process. These are examples of the types of support you might be able to offer:

- Direct and specific professional or technical support to their project or general encouragement for their CHERISH project.
- A means of enabling or directly providing knowledge exchange relating to your project and theirs, perhaps involving the exchange of comparison data.
- Support as a critical friend to CHERISH project leaders, CHERISH Champions and staff, perhaps involving use of some of your own staff in the delivery of learning.
- Presenting your own achievements to those involved in the supported organisation to demonstrate the benefits of undertaking a CHERISH project.
- Relationship-building advice between staff, contractors and other stakeholders who may only recently have been brought together to undertake the project.
- Advice on how to act as an organisational conduit for spreading the word about CHERISH.
- Advice on the make-up of CHERISH groups, skillsets, decision-making and governance.

But do remember that you are not responsible for the delivery of the project you are helping to support. The host organisation must be responsible for their own delivery and therefore aware that they need to monitor progress as they would for any other project. Your role is to offer help, guidance and your learning.

You will need to plan how and when you can provide help to your supported organisation so that you do not jeopardise your own service and its improvement. Just as they always advise you on airlines, 'make sure you secure your own oxygen mask before assisting others'.

Since the CHERISH process is iterative, both organisations should ensure they schedule natural 'taking stock' points in to the help you are providing and specify the expected outputs from this stocktaking. An open dialogue will make the most of your time and you will want to ensure the organisation you are supporting is obtaining value from your contribution. There is nothing worse than agreeing to a programme only to find several weeks in that neither of you understood the other and you are working to different agendas.

Ideally, your plan will include a clear timetable and specific monitoring outcomes for the progress of the project. It will set out decisively what the mutual expectations are, and the commitment needed from both sides. It can be amended as you go along, of course, but it should also be able to serve as a reference and a reminder to participants, and perhaps also as a 'calling card' for future organisations if both parties are willing to share it. Drawing up such a plan will also help you consider how much time you can afford to devote to helping other projects. If you have decided that you can spare, say, four half days per month to help a project, and you set this down in advance in the plan and schedule the dates, there will be less temptation for the other organisation to ask for more than this.

What should I expect from my chosen organisation?

Above all, the organisation you are helping should be willing to be helped, and should be able to demonstrate that they can commit the time, resources and crucially, the senior management backing necessary to capitalise on your offer.

Also, to put it bluntly, the organisation needs to be in a fit state to take on the challenge. If you are an upper-quartile organisation, do you really want to take on a degree of responsibility for a lower-quartile organisation? In the age of austerity, misplaced effort is a luxury no one can afford. But if one of the aims of your organisation is to help and partner those below you in the performance stakes, be prepared to tailor your offer to what they can realistically achieve.

You may have to treat candidate organisations in a similar way to how the EU treats candidate accession countries. They need to be able to demonstrate certain hallmarks of civil society to be eligible for entry, such as a level of democracy, a functioning criminal justice system, etc. Likewise, you may have to specify the degree of commitment and a minimum level of resources that are your prerequisites for taking on these organisations. The 'Help' stage of CHERISH could in fact be a rolling programme, so those who are not taken on immediately should not view this as outright failure. Even the pointers you provide as to the standards for eligibility will constitute a benefit for them.

One of the biggest challenges in helping other organisations is maintaining their focus on action and delivery. It is all so much easier where you have a direct input through line management, but you will have to exercise a form of dispersed leadership to sustain progress in other organisations. This will be perhaps a new experience for you, acting as an advocate and adviser in an organisation in which you have no management responsibility – it could make for interesting learning for you!

There is probably – hopefully, even – no organisation so dysfunctional that it has absolutely nothing to offer in terms of learning from its way of doing things. Organisations may be struggling with one particular aspect of their operations, but at the same time it is highly likely that in working with them you will identify insights unavailable elsewhere. Ideally, you will have been upfront about selecting your host organisation on the basis of the mutual learning to be had from your assistance. Building processes to support the development of learning into the plan, such as regular exchange of documents, sharing of assessment results, etc. will make sure that valuable and timely information is not lost.

How will I know if I have got there?

This is a tricky one. Applying a hard-and-fast tool like a performance management framework is obviously not going to work in this more diffuse type of support activity, though that it is not to say that managers within the host organisations should not be applying them. You will be looking to capture some of the softer intelligence from this exercise, and considering what some of the intangible benefits might be.

A successful partnership between you and your chosen organisation(s) should yield an enormous amount of useful information – useful not only for you and for your opposite numbers, but useful for anyone in the public sector. If that information can be organised or packaged in a way that can be reused, then that is a significant step forward. Such a resource will provide evidence of the effectiveness of the CHERISH programme and of the public sector taking the austerity challenge head on. It can be hard to second-guess what people might want to see in such a resource, but I have provided an outline checklist at www.newpublicsector.com that you can use as a starting point. You will also find the most recent examples of shared experiences and offers of help and support from others who have been through the CHERISH journey.

Developing constructive relationships with the host sites underpins everything. If you can honestly answer 'yes' to at least some of the following questions, you can be confident that you have developed a positive relationship with them that will deliver mutual benefits:

- Am I meeting with the sites regularly, as agreed?
- Are staff and stakeholders from the site participating fully in the CHERISH forum?
- Is there a high degree of trust and honesty between me and the sites?
- Would the sites I am working with recommend the process to others?
- Are both parties happy with the outcomes being delivered?
- Are other public sector organisations starting to approach me to ask me about my experiences?
- Have my own message management systems picked up from my audience that my service is so good that it is helping others?
- Have I made sure that our support to other services is properly understood by my audience and my organisation?
- Am I/is my organisation receiving positive feedback?

You could even consider using these questions as a standing agenda item at your regular meetings, to provide an opportunity for dialogue about these vital issues. If you want to use this as a launchpad for the next iteration of the CHERISH process for your own service, the information you glean by being part of a wider change network is likely to benefit and influence your own work. I would suggest that you are getting there when you have supported five services other than your own through the CHERISH process.

Finally, what narratives are circulating about the process, both within the host organisations and outside? Again, social media monitoring, local press and staff meetings can provide valuable in-sights from a range of perspectives, and if the narrative is one of enthusiasm, or even cautious acceptance (as opposed to catch-all moaning!), you will know you have made a contribution.

CHAPTER 4

What If I Don't Bother?

What this chapter covers

The title of this chapter is self-explanatory: it describes the likely implications of you not attending to the demands of the austerity agenda and not bothering to prepare yourself or your service for the demands of the New Public Sector. While it is your decision whether to bother, I am guessing that you have read this far because you do care about your future.

Not bothering is a perfectly legitimate option, but you do need to be aware of the possible consequences and to consider what you will do if austerity comes knocking and you have not prepared yourself or your service.

As I was completing *How to Survive Austerity* on 25 November 2015, the Government published the results of the Spending Review, setting out how £4 trillion of taxpayers' money will be spent on government departments and public services like the NHS and schools. I highlighted the main conclusions of that review earlier in *How to Survive Austerity* so you would understand the reality of what the public sector faces in the years ahead. The high level summary of that review was a reduction in public sector funding of some £20 billion per annum, coupled with additional efficiency targets for some departments that had negotiated their own arrangements.

Much was made in the press leading up to the review's conclusion about the various wrangles and the positioning each department was involved in. The results of these discussions are the departmental settlements – the amount the Government has allocated to each department to spend over the Parliament. Departmental budgets can be spent on the running of the services that they oversee, such as schools or hospitals, but also on the everyday cost of resources such as staff.

As I outlined right at the start of *How to Survive Austerity*, the Government updates its plans for the economy twice a year, at the time of the Budget and of the Autumn Statement. The Autumn Statement usually happens in November or December, the Budget in March, ahead of the new financial year. In 2015, the Spending Review and Autumn Statement were combined.

As I watched the Chancellor explaining how he has allocated the public's money, I was struck by the percentage reductions being distributed across the various spending departments. Some departments' budgets were ring-fenced, meaning that others needed to pick up a larger share of the overall reductions required by the austerity drive. I was also struck by the monetary sums attached to those percentages. And I understood just what that would mean for many public sector organisations and services up and down the land.

By way of a snapshot, and ahead of the Chancellor's announcement, a survey of hospital finance directors by the Healthcare Financial Management Association found that 100% of respondents expected to end the year in deficit, up from 77% in July 2015. Just as worrying, a significant proportion of those same finance directors did not believe the £22 billion efficiency savings set out in the NHS Five Year Forward View are achievable on current plans and assumptions. A number of reports (also issued before the Chancellor's announcement) pointed to adult social care being in an equally perilous state, predicting a potential funding gap of £6 billion by 2020/21 even before factoring in the costs for care providers of implementing the mandatory National Living Wage. Leaving aside any pre-announcement positioning, such concerns reflect genuine worries and provide a focus on the sustainability of such core parts of our public services.

If ever there was a reason to consider doing something rather than nothing, reading and understanding the Chancellor's statement on 25 November 2015, and the Office of Budget Responsibility (OBR) report that accompanied his speech, would be it. I recommend you read the OBR's report at www.budgetresponsibility.org.uk

'Cherish' rhymes with 'Perish'

Before we look at a summary of what you have ahead of you courtesy of the 2015 Spending Review and consider the implications for you and your service, it is worth reflecting on the extent to which we have explored how austerity will affect your service and the public you serve.

You will recall that we considered what you could do to minimise that impact, or at least to demonstrate to those who are driving the austerity agenda what you have done to ensure your service is relevant to the public and offers good value for money. I have also been clear throughout *How to Survive Austerity* that despite your best efforts, all that hard work may still come to nothing.

You will remember also the reasons I chose CHERISH as the name for this improvement process, and the definitions for some of the component parts. You may also remember that I said I liked the fact that CHERISH rhymes with PERISH, and that I used the notion of gladiators, 'thumbs up' and 'thumbs down', and an 'Arena of Austerity' to convey the idea of public services being CHERISHed by the public. The association of a 'thumbs down' with PERISHing is simple and strong. The extent of change in the public sector required following the Spending Review will cast that gladiatorial idea into sharp focus.

We also considered whether your service could be dispensed with in one fell swoop, or could die the death of a thousand cuts after being salami-sliced to the point where it can no longer function. Looking at the outcome of the Spending Review, salami-slicing may no longer be able to deliver the cuts required. It is far more likely that entire units and areas of work will go, and in this context only the service that is identified as being valued and delivering with maximum efficiency stands a chance. And 'stands a chance' may be as about as good as it gets. There are no guarantees here. Not doing anything is going to maximise your likelihood of being at risk. Doing something will at least minimise it.

So against that fairly grim backdrop, there is bound to be a temptation simply to roll over and let whatever is coming your way happen. It is human nature sometimes to pick the 'flight' option. It goes back to our primitive beginnings based on intuitive behaviour. The issue for you, then, as a public sector manager, is to decide which of these options is right for you in the face of the threat of austerity.

My proposition is a simple one. I want you to make an effort, to look at what you do and improve it, and to engage with the public and seek their approval through their CHERISHing your service. I would argue that making that effort and those improvements is the right thing for public services, and that you should be doing this anyway. I would argue that going that extra mile and seeking the approval and the passionate commitment of the public is something all public services will need to do in the emerging New Public Sector. Having evidence of engagement and improvement will help your cause when the reduced level of public spending starts to bite. But what I think does not really matter. *What really matters is what you think.*

I have assumed throughout *How to Survive Austerity* that you have spent some time delivering public services and have at least a degree of passion for the concept of the public sector. While you may not live and breathe public services, you are aligned with their ethos and recognise the importance of providing high quality, cost-effective services to the UK public. Your service may be local, regional or national; it could collect taxation or other income; it could pay out money to people or businesses that need it; or it could deliver vital services without which our society would not function – whichever of these it is, you clearly subscribe to the necessity of having good public services.

Given that, you need to decide if you want to go through the steps I have outlined in the CHERISH process or simply roll over and not bother. Be aware that if you do not bother, what may happen is that someone will come along and say 'You know what? This is a service that is not supported, that is not valued by anybody, so no one will shed any tears if we cut it.' Simple as that.

I have described a process I am happy to characterise as a 'not rocket science' approach, using existing techniques to deliver a fairly common-sense outcome. It is important to remember that we are not talking about one of those interminable change programmes that seem to get dragged under by organisational inertia. I am quite sure we can all point to change programmes that seem to grind to a halt without having delivered very much. With CHERISH, we are talking about a twelve-week programme to identify and initiate concrete practical action – you are not signing your life away.

And CHERISH offers a very simple way for organisations to undertake a whole-service review. The building blocks are not complex and each service has an opportunity to showcase ways it can improve and engage better with its audience, all within twelve weeks. I am not sure there are many other processes that would even have completed their initial set-up steps within that time, so it is very effective to implement.

But consider the alternatives to doing something proactive. What options are open to public sector managers who decide that the effort is not for them? What if you just prefer to sit and ride out the current wave of austerity? Have another look for yourself at the main features of the 2015 Spending Review and see what not doing anything at all may deliver to your doorstep.

Can I outrun austerity?

In a word, no. There are no parts of the public sector that are immune to austerity, efficiency and a downward trend in spending. Even special cases like defence, health, and education all have their own efficiency plans. Flagship hospitals, for example, can be put into special measures, demonstrating just how inescapable the tentacles of austerity are.

I hardly need to tell you that cuts to public services are nothing new. We have always had cuts, and many say that the extent of budget reductions was more severe in relative terms in the 1970s. But as we have noted, reductions and belt tightening have generally been followed by some kind of 'public sector reflation' when the economy reaches a better point in the economic cycle. This time it looks and feels different.

What I am inviting you to do is to take at least some form of control even if you do not have total control. Do not wait until someone comes around asking you to cut this and cut that, at which point you will have to scramble to arrange this on the basis of expediency rather than on the basis of a considered assessment of what is best for your service. You have at least a window of opportunity, and it would be remiss of you not to make the most of it.

However inspiring the bounce-back in the private sector may prove to be, we are unlikely to see any great diversion of funds to the public sector in the future. The ethos has changed for good. The emerging New Public Sector will mean public services and the way they are viewed will be different in future. The alternative to action – keeping your head down and hoping retirement comes along to save you – seems a little weak, although some may be in that position. The wider economy will offer employment opportunities to many currently working in the public sector but not all. You need to try to be one of those emerging to lead the New Public Sector.

Perhaps what I am saying, simply put, is that it is better to go down fighting!

CHAPTER 5

Spreading the Message

What this chapter covers

We have reached the end of *How to Survive Austerity*, but you are not at the end of your journey to become CHERISHed. In fact, if it is not too much of a cliché, you are just at the start of your journey.

I would imagine you have read *How to Survive Austerity* pretty quickly and that you may have liked some of the ideas in the book – maybe you liked all the ideas, which is even better. You may have thought as you were reading, 'Yes, I could apply that to my service' or perhaps, 'Yes, I can see the benefits of engaging with my public to get a better understanding of what they want.'

But I cannot imagine that, by this stage, you will have completed your CHERISH journey – not on the first reading of it, anyway. So this is the part of the book where I tell you to:

- Think about what you have read and make a decision to do something.
- Go back and read each chapter again so you can map out what that 'something' is for your service.
- Visit the various online references I have provided, particularly www.newpublicsector.com, and see what updated information

I have shared and what additional frameworks, templates and material are already there for you to use.

- Start planning the CHERISH journey for your service and make sure others in your organisation are aware of what you are doing.

This last point is perhaps the most important. We have already established that you cannot deliver a CHERISH programme in glorious isolation. You need to engage many others, not hide away. We have explored the parts of your organisation and your network you must engage with. We have identified the actions you must undertake to gain rapid traction to *do something* to meet the challenges of austerity. So make a promise to yourself to engage others and share the messages you have gleaned from *How to Survive Austerity*, so there are more people you can converse with on your own journey.

That sharing should be pan-sector, not restricted only to your own organisation or professional network. The conclusions of the November 2015 Spending Review make sober reading, no matter which part of the public sector or part of the country you are in. There will be few areas of the public sector not impacted, either directly or indirectly, by austerity and the Spending Review. Local and central government will be affected, as will the devolved government arrangements that are already a key part of the pattern of the UK public sector and look set to increase as greater powers are passed to devolved bodies across the country. It seems that at a time when budgets are being cut, there is an increased need for more local bodies to assume responsibility for delivery.

There will be plenty of people who are in the same boat as you – some you know already, some you do not yet know, but you will not be short of people to engage with to share your experiences. As you share your experiences, you become better known across the public sector, and being better known for positive change is generally, in my experience, a good thing. In sharing the message, you will serve your own interests as well as those of the public sector – well, there has to be some personal reward for all your hard work.

Tell it like it is

The key message from this final section is to make sure you spread the CHERISH message, making it clear that this is an approach that does not involve 'rocket science'. This is a personal passion of mine: I like to apply straightforward, common-sense thinking to everything I do. Well, most things anyway!

I cannot imagine there will be many medals given out for developing and promoting a public sector improvement methodology that costs millions to apply, months to set up and many staff hours to implement. Aim to get your 'share message' across by focusing on the simplicity of the first three CHERISH stages: Clarity, How Much? and Evaluate. I do not think that suggesting to people that the public sector should pitch its services to the public, reduce costs and measure those costs against the best in class will raise many hackles, so focus on that as a core message. You can add more detail once people have bought into the concept.

Once you have gone through the CHERISH process yourself, you will become what is commonly called an expert. You will have gained expertise that many other people do not have and will have acquired learning from your experience. You may have to go through several iterations yourself to gain that CHERISHed status, and each time you will gain more experience. Others will be able to look to you for advice and guidance on their own journeys. It is part of the public sector ethos to share experiences with others, and it is certainly in the public interest that you advocate on behalf of the process and declare, 'I went through a simple improvement process and it was good for my service.'

Every public sector manager should at least look at the CHERISH process and consider how effective such a simple seven-step approach can be. You can be part of supporting widespread improvement if you share you own experience. In addition to adopting a target for yourself to support five peer organisations through their CHERISH journey, you should aim to share the approach across the public sector. It would be a great achievement to propel such a practical approach into common use and make sure all public sector managers understand the importance of ensuring their service is CHERISHed. And of course, do feel free to refer them to *How to Survive Austerity*!

But it will not be all plain sailing. The demands of austerity are relentless and if by any chance you are reading this book in 2020, you will know just how hard those demands have been. In sharing the message, whether you are addressing an internal or an external audience, I would suggest you do not gloss over hard messages. The austerity journey will be tough, the outcomes will be hard and not everyone will survive the journey. People within the public sector and outside it have frankly heard the message enough times now to get used to the realities of austerity. Not everyone agrees with the roadmap of austerity and not everyone agrees with the overall outcome, but there can be few who are not aware something is going on with their public services. Be honest about what you can achieve and the extent to which you can resist the tide of change.

The trick is to craft your sharing messages in such a way that they do not provoke antagonism against those who have seen their services extended or maintained at the expense of others, focusing perhaps on the benefits to the community overall. Internally, your own colleagues and stakeholders need to know that the CHERISH process is unlikely to be pain-free, but that the aim is to make their service valued by their public, client or audience. It is not a process that seeks to make life a bed of roses for those who deliver it.

But your directness, fortunately, will help those you are sharing with to be succinct in formulating their pitch, as we learned earlier in the CHERISH process. Once you have gone through your own process and learned the power of a 30-second pitch of your service, you will be able to articulate that power much more readily to others who have not.

A warning – I am not advocating you transform into a wild-eyed Ancient Mariner pouncing on everyone you come across and ear-bashing them with your message of salvation. I suspect you will only put them off.

Sharing opportunities

You will have your own range of platforms and opportunities you can exploit to share your journey and the CHERISH process. As ever, you are best placed to decide what these are and how you want to get your message across. Some of these sharing opportunities will be internal to your own organisation, such as peer meetings, management meetings and staff engagement, while others will be external, such as professional networks, conferences, service-related social media and articles. There will be many opportunities to engage with stakeholders, the public, clients and your wider audience during the CHERISH process itself. The fact that you have gone through the process is likely to mean that you will have a wider and more in-depth network than before you started. Do not be afraid to use that network and share the message of the technique you used to engage your audience. You will be surprised at how many people will be keen to learn more and will, in turn, share what you did with others.

You could make use of informal chats with colleagues, maybe the presentation of a detailed case study at a conference, place eye-catching snippets of information about your project on your Twitter account or a relevant Facebook page, or maybe prepare an online article or blog. This could be particularly useful for providing advice on how you have overcome specific difficulties, as everyone is always interested in hearing about how people solved a problem they perhaps have themselves.

In fact, the options for sharing will be bounded only by your own imagination. To support you in the process, I have set up a range of information exchanges on www.newpublicsector.com. These include:

- Requests for help from those just starting their CHERISH journey.
- Offers of support from those further along on their journey.
- The Arena of Austerity, so that you can see how others have presented themselves and how the public has reacted.
- Tips, hints and material you can use as well as material provided by others who have been happy to share what they learned and developed during their own CHERISH journeys.
- Up-to-date information on the latest in austerity news.

There are numerous other online options and sources of information, and the online resource will provide access to all those I find. Please feel free to add more, because there is nothing better than free-shared resources.

If you are starting out on the CHERISH journey, the online resource will provide guidance, and hopefully an assurance that, whatever the pitfalls you encounter, there is someone else out there who has gone before, overcome the barriers and survived to tell the tale. If you are a CHERISH veteran, it is in your gift to contribute your valuable experience to this resource, but you will also be able to tap into the myriad of different perspectives of those working in different cultures, satisfying different demands.

But evangelism is more than merely contributing to a website on a personal basis. Ideally you will be taking every opportunity to tell people your own CHERISH story. People like a good story and there are few better ways of engaging people than telling them yours. On the formal side, you will no doubt be being asked to report back at meetings or perhaps to give presentations at meetings, all of which offers you a chance to update people on the progress of CHERISH projects. If you can find a hook on which to hang your stories, so much the better. It may be that you can match your narrative to the issues preoccupying your organisation at any given time.

And do not overlook what the CHERISH Champions have to offer. Within your own organisation, it will provide corroboration of your experience, but perhaps from a different, or even a more junior, perspective, which will give it credibility. The CHERISH Champions can also advise you on the shifting concerns within your organisation, which your narrative could address. External champions should be able to give you a wider view, enabling some horizon scanning on your part, which will help you to be flexible and to anticipate future challenges.

Find your level

A word of warning I am sure you do not need but I will give it anyway!

Beware of the risk of taking on too much or tackling the wrong thing. The last thing you want to do is PERISH through a misguided attempt to overreach yourself, or focus on an issue or task that diverts your attention away from the actual risk and challenge. Make sure you focus your efforts on the problem in hand, not one you want to address or like tackling. Nero, Rome, fire and fiddling come to mind!

There is also a balance between taking no action and trying to do too much. You want to avoid opting for targets or aiming to address issues that will do no more than make a rod for your own back, commit to savings that you just will not be able to deliver or solve problems that are not fundamental.

The demands of the New Public Sector will mean you must become much more attuned to the real issues, now, in front of your eyes, today, even more than you have been in the past.

So you must be absolutely clear about the position in your own organisation. What did the 2015 Spending Review do for you? What priorities need to change? What fundamentals have shifted? What are budgets now and what are they likely to be in the future? What role does your organisation want you to play in making those changes?

It will be important that you find the most appropriate level for you, given all those issues. You need to develop your proactiveness and thrust yourself forward as one of those the organisation can rely on to deliver, rather than stand idly by and let things simply happen to you. You need to position yourself as far as you can as a 'go-to' person who can be relied on to deliver, to stand up and be counted – many clichés, I know, but you get the point.

Be aware of developments and shifts in the culture of your organisation. Do not rely on existing preconceptions of how things are. Large and complex organisations such as the NHS, for example, no longer have a single, coherent organisational culture. The NHS is now many organisations, each with its own agendas and cultures. All NHS bodies share patient care as a core value, but their day-to-day cultures and the way they do business are different, and a local authority in Scotland or Manchester is likely to have a vastly different organisational culture and context from a local authority in London.

Only you can really judge whether it will be possible, for example, to deliver a project that will result in large savings in one area of your organisation at the expense of another. How would your organisation react to such a plan? What kind of delivery process would that involve and what form would the political (small 'p') advocacy take? And, more importantly, how will your organisation react next month and in six months' time, when austerity starts to bite? Perhaps you understood what the organisation would do in the past, but make sure you recognise what it will do today or tomorrow. Find that organisational level for yourself and make sure you keep attuned to the changes that are happening.

Above all, I suggest you make sure you get involved in the right debates, so you understand the things you need to understand. Your time is too precious for you to be dragged into discussion, debates and projects that are ultimately not critical to the future success of your service.

Just as the messages change, so too your own ways of sharing success will need to change. It will be difficult, and keeping your head will be half the battle. We are all aware of the extent of spending reductions agreed in the 2015 Spending Review. Big and scary austerity attracts more viewers, sells many more papers and achieves many more hits for online news services. Make sure you hone your sharing messages as things change. If you have been using the same message for more than three months, it is probably time you changed it or at least had a close look at its continued relevance. Last but certainly not least, make sure you are delivering a message that is consistent with the ethos and direction of your organisation and that you check regularly for alignment.

CHERISH fatigue and the next big thing

As we draw to the close of *How to Survive Austerity*, I must add a word about the endless round of new 'faddy' initiatives, successive change programmes, and the 'next big thing'. It does need to be addressed.

You know the drill: new whizz-bang techniques and processes are brought in with a big fanfare. Everyone rushes around doing a lot of 'stuff'. Then, as often as not, nothing is followed through. It all goes quiet and in a year another one comes along, and people think, 'Hang on a second, what happened to the previous one?'

Well, I have worked in the public service for many years and the private sector before that, so I have seen my fair share of efficiency and improvement techniques come and go. Aside from the application of technology, most of those techniques applied basic common sense and improvement methodologies based on 'old-fashioned' approaches that have been around for decades, even if they are increasingly packaged in a way calculated to appeal to our complex organisations. Complex organisational problems need complex solutions, goes the argument.

Given the scale of the austerity agenda, there will certainly need to be strong programme management, to drive forward service cessation, service reduction, service change and service efficiency programmes. Despite the scale of that change, the programmes must still have a degree of equity and rigour applied to them. The 2015 Spending Review has set the policy framework for budget reductions and departmental efficiencies; it is now down to individual spending bodies to determine how best they can meet those challenges.

Against that background, you need to be very clear that CHERISH is nothing more than:

- The application of common sense and planning you should already be doing.
- A logical deployment of actions that are already familiar to most people, rather than the invention of new ones.
- A concise process designed specifically for public services trying to make sense of the very pressing problem austerity has delivered to our collective doorstep.

It does not purport to be 'the next big thing', although there may well be a new 'big thing' along, fashioned to meet the needs of the public sector at this time of significant challenge. Watch out for these and treat them with caution. Pursue what your organisation has decided you will do, working within the delivery constraints and using whatever tools the technique gives you to maximise its value.

I would advocate that you rely on applying common sense to what is a very basic, if very large, problem. The emerging New Public Sector will dictate what form public services need to take in future. The challenges of mismatched demand and supply will need to be addressed. You will only have so much budget to deliver so much service; ideally, new and innovative partnerships and ways of working will emerge. There is nothing really new in any of that, other than maybe the pace of change and the impact it will have on people's lives.

So when you are developing your approach to meeting the challenges of austerity and deciding how you can best position yourself and your service to meet the challenges of the New Public Sector, please bear that in mind. Simple messages are best for:

- Sharing and communicating your messages so you leave no confusion in the minds of those you are engaging.
- Developing clarity on what you do.
- Reducing your costs to the lowest feasible level.
- Asking the public to consider the evidence you present to them.
- Getting other people to do the same.

It is as simple as that.

One thing is for sure, though: anyone reading *How to Survive Austerity* in 2020 will be able to judge for themselves how relevant the challenge still is. The truth of the matter is that something else may happen along in the next few years that will become the new focus of attention, but the skills and experience that you have acquired through your CHERISH efforts will never be wasted.

In fact, if you have a good idea about where CHERISH could go next, get in touch and let me know! I am certainly going to be giving it some thought.

And Finally ...

If you are still with me, very well done!

I suspect you may be about to take on the CHERISH challenge, and I would like to wish you best of luck every step of the way. May you find supportive sponsors and enthusiastic champions to match your ambition and energy and to help you get the best out of the process.

Do not be shy about asking me any questions you may have about any aspect of the CHERISH process or about anything I have said in *How to Survive Austerity*. I would love to hear from you.

If you have any queries or observations, want to make contact with me or others who are on the same journey, do not hesitate to join the conversation at www.newpublicsector.com. Lots of free no-nonsense material, help and support are available for you there.

The revolution may be quiet, but I am sure the consequences will be life changing.

And remember my favourite saying: 'Common sense is not that common.'

Good luck!

Acknowledgements

It is a great feeling to have both started and finished a book but there are many, many people I need to thank for their help, support and inspiration. I would first like to thank all those clients, colleagues and partners I have met over the years who have given me so much food for thought, inspiration and passion. The learning we went through together is woven into the words of this book. You may even recognise some of those words as your own.

Next, there are so many people who have helped me complete this book and I am sorry if I have missed you off this list. I must first thank my good friend Jim Brooks for agreeing to write a foreword for my book and to the many people who contributed to my research. I will say particular thanks to Fraser McK, Alice B, James P, Janine W, John W, Andy V, Martin S, David A, Pete W and eagle-eyed Tom. And special thanks to Lucy Gower, Daniel Priestley and Phil Trickey for allowing me to reproduce their most excellent thoughts and words from their publications.

Much appreciation must go to my Libre colleagues, Rachel, Dale and Ken, for their patience and tolerance of my occasional ranting over the past few months. I can only say this is likely to continue.

And big thanks to those people who have, and continue to, use their expertise and insight to bring my book to life and make me look good. My booksmith, Verity, was so patient and supportive during the writing process, for which major thanks. And of course Lucy and Joe are the only people I would ever recommend if you want to write and publish a book. You guys are simply wonderful. And a very special thanks to Sapna and Sarah who have done such a great job on my graphics, website and social media. And to those of you who kindly provided praise for my book (and for reading it before it looks as good as it does now), many thanks. If your quote is not in the book it surely will be on the website.

And finally and most importantly, massive thanks to, and appreciation of, my partner Mandy's considerable patience whilst I was writing this first book and for her sharp-sighted proof reading skills in the final edit. You are a star.

The Author

Mike is a business change consultant who has worked in the public sector for more than 25 years. He started his career working as an industrial engineer and performance manager in his native North East of England. He moved to Scotland in 1989 and has worked across the UK public sector ever since on projects that seek to deliver 'more for less'.

Mike's passion is for developing sustainable improvement in public services and for joining up things that are not currently joined up. Over the course of his career, Mike has gained great understanding of the nature of public services as well as the people who work in them. He has a deep knowledge of the importance of realising improvements and efficiencies as well as the process needed to ensure their delivery.

Mike is a partner in Libre Advisory, a consulting company he started in 2000 to focus on public service improvement. Mike has helped improve public-facing services in health, local government, police and central government as well as working on strategic change, back-office and shared service programmes.

Mike has a wholehearted belief in a strong public sector delivering high quality services at a cost comparable with the private sector. Austerity has ignited Mike's desire to help public sector managers maximise their chances of survival and he has established a website to provide further advice on *How To Survive Austerity*. You can find that advice at www.newpublicsector.com and you can Link-In with Mike at www.linkedin.com/in/mikegill62 or visit him at Libre's website, www.libre.co.uk.

Printed in Great Britain
by Amazon

35480646R00098